T0106106

YOU WENT WHERE?

An Unexpected Journey to Cameroon

WARREN PERRY

ILLUSTRATIONS BY LORNA HOOVER

iUniverse, Inc.
Bloomington

YOU WENT WHERE?
An Unexpected Journey to Cameroon

iUniverse books may be ordered through booksellers or by contacting:

iUniverse
1663 Liberty Drive
Bloomington, IN 47403
www.iuniverse.com
1-800-Authors (1-800-288-4677)

ISBN: 978-1-4759-6384-7 (sc)
ISBN: 978-1-4759-6385-4 (ebk)

Library of Congress Control Number: 2012922413

Printed in the United States of America

iUniverse rev. date: 03/14/2013

You Went Where?

CONTENTS

Ch 1   I answer Lorna's ad 1
Ch 2   Harvard Square to Bologna 5
Ch 3   We decide to go to Wum...12
Ch 4   First days in Cameroon 21
Ch 5   Train to the far north..31
Ch 6   N'Gaoundere to Garoua...37
Ch 7   Maroua, Lake Maga, & Chad.....................................44
Ch 8   Waza, Rhumsiki, and the Maribout.........................53
Ch 9   Return to Buea 62
Ch 10   Daily life in Buea..67
Ch 11   We flee to Bamenda 75
Ch 12   Thievery and friendship 85
Ch 13   Paul's Computer School 94
Ch 14   The Fondom of Bafut...102
Ch 15   We finally get to Wum 106
Ch 16   "Kidnapped" 113
Ch 17   We meet Robert Graham..120
Ch 18   Bali, Foumban, farewell Bamenda 127
Ch 19   Farewell Buea and Cameroon 135
Postscript   Some unfinished business...141

GUIDE TO PRONOUNCIATIONS

Bafoussam	—	bah-foo'-sam
Buea	—	boy' yah
Douala	—	doo ah' lah
Foumban	—	foom' bahn
Garoua	—	gah roo' ah
Guider	—	gee' day
Limbe	—	lim' bay
Maroua	—	mah roo' ah
N'Gaoundere	—	gown' derr ay
Wum	—	whoom'
Yaounde	—	yah oon' day

CAMEROON

Railroad

100 mi

CHAD

KOUSSÉRI

MORA

Manoua

moKolo

NIGERIA

GUIDER

tchellire

BANYO

Ngaoundéré

CENTRAL

wum

NKAMBE

AFRICAN

BARMENDA

REPUBLIC

GAROUA
Bouli

BELABO

MOUNT CAMEROON

MONATÉLÉ

DOUALA

MALABO

EDÉA

Youndi

YOKADOUMA

Kribi

AKOM

SANG-MÉLIMA

EQUATORIAL

GUINEA

GABON

CONGO

CH 1

I answer Lorna's ad

Jessie

My sister once thought I was an adventurer because I went off to London without making my hotel reservations in advance. "What if you can't find a room?" she worried.

"Well then, I suppose I would have to sleep on the grass in Hyde Park, or sleep on the floor in Victoria Station."

"You're not twenty years old anymore."

"And we're not talking about the heart of Africa."

My children, I am sure, agreed with her. I was retired and lived alone in the house where they had grown up. My wife had died a few years earlier, barely six months after we had retired from our antique business and I was left to deal alone with the leftovers of nearly forty years. It was too much to think about. An eclectic mass of leftovers from sales and auctions had slowly grown from year to year until my

1

attic, cellar, garage, and the unused rooms that our children had vacated were filled. I confined myself to the habitable rooms and shut the door to the past. I was depressed.

I had never exercised much, but now, out of boredom, I began walking every day in some woods near where I lived. I always took along my dog Jessie, a small, 5-year old black Lab that at that time in my life was my constant and only companion. Initially, I found it was hard to walk even a mile, but within a few weeks, I was able to walk 4 or 5 miles at a time, and do it every day at a pace that I would not have previously thought possible. I decided to make walking a permanent feature of my life and tried to never miss a day. I walked in heavy rain, deep snow, and subzero temperatures, and on days that my resolution failed, Jessie never allowed me to fail. There were days that I was so tired that I didn't think it was possible to move, but Jessie would sit and watch me expectantly until she had caught my attention, and then race back and forth to the front door, all the while barking, until I struggled to my feet and headed for the front door. As my stamina improved, depression disappeared. It was impossible for me to walk and feel depressed at the same time and I felt better than I had in years.

There is a Latin saying, '*Mens sana in corpore sano*'—a sound mind in a sound body. I now turned my attention to my brain. There are people who take up bridge, or do crossword puzzles to keep their minds sharp. I decided that I would learn French. I had taken two years of French in high school, but I hadn't been especially keen on it. I had preferred to spend my time on science and math courses that I enjoyed more. Now, so many years later, French was exactly what I needed, a new parallel language network to offset any decline that could begin to establish itself in my brain.

I began with the preparation of dozens of 3x5 index cards to use for vocabulary practice during my rambles through the woods. I pronounced the words aloud and made up sentences as I walked. Jessie often turned and looked at me quizzically, unsure about whether or not my French was directed toward her. During the next few years, I went to the University of Quebec on two occasions for three-week immersion courses in the French language. I also subscribed to TV5 for French television, and bought what became a small library of French literature. I especially enjoyed a subscription to "Paris Match", a photojournal that kept me abreast events in France.

I had never been to France, but travel there was now, definitely, on my agenda. In early October of 2000, I finally embarked on a long solo trip that lasted until just before Christmas of that year. I visited almost every part of the country from Normandy to Nice and from Strasbourg to the Mediterranean coast near Spain. I began my trip with two weeks of study at a language school in Southwest France. My classmates there were a congenial group of people from The United States and Canada, one of whom was a retired radiologist from Washington D.C. named Gunther who had been my classmate at the University in Quebec. We had shared an apartment there and had been good friends. We had each come to France alone and were surprised and pleased to meet up again. Our French classes consisted of periods of instruction followed by visits to castles, prehistoric caves, markets, and private homes throughout Lot and Dordogne. Our meals were superb. Lunches were leisurely and could take as long as two hours. Dinners usually took up our entire evenings.

When the course ended, most of our classmates flew home from Bordeaux, the closest major city. Gunther went off to visit family and friends in Germany while I took a train to Paris. I spent a week there. It was not enough time to devote to one of the loveliest cities in the world, but I wanted see the entire country. In the weeks that followed, I explored Normandy, Alsace-Lorraine, Burgundy, Provence, and Languedoc, by train and by rental car. I drove through the Pyrenees mountains, visited the tiny nation of Andorra, and sampled the wines of the countryside.

My sister's fears were finally realized one evening in Toulouse after I had returned my rental car. A trade fair had filled all the hotels and sleeping on the floor of the train station became a real possibility. However, I decided to use my rail pass and I took an overnight train going to Nice. I only stayed for a single night in Nice, but I was tired of carrying my luggage around and left it in a locker at the RR station while I went for a few days to Dijon and Avignon. That was a mistake because the train trip to retrieve it was much longer than I had expected and to reach Lyon, my final destination, I had to make the long journey twice.

In Lyon, I rented a room in an apartment owned by an attractive widow who charged me very little money. She was a poet and had also taught school for many years in Morocco. When I informed her that I was trying to improve my French, she stopped using English entirely, in her conversations with me. Every morning at breakfast, we planned possible itineraries for my explorations of that day. In the evening when I returned, usually after dining at some restaurant that she had recommended, we talked about my impressions of what I had seen, and we often ended the day reading some of our favorite poetry aloud. I flew home from Lyon after more than two months in France. I had really missed my dog, Jessie. She was delighted to see me when I came back and I felt so guilty for having left her at a kennel that I let her to sleep on my bed after that.

I was disappointed with my human friends. I came back bursting with stories to tell about the trip, but they had all become so busy and involved in one affair or another that no one had the time to listen to my travel tales. I consoled myself with long solitary walks in the woods with Jessie.

The first Sunday of the New Year was also the first Sunday of both a new century and a new millennium. I was desultorily sifting through the pages of the Boston Sunday Globe and sipping my third cup of coffee when the words, "coffee, conversation" caught my eye. They were in a personal ad, and I stopped to read it:

> Coffee, conversation, music, seeking warm friendship, Boston Area, with romantic person in 60's who loves foreign travel.

Impulsively I decided to meet the woman who had written the ad. I followed the instructions given in the column and left a voice message on her telephone. I learned her name was Lorna when she called me the next day. She suggested that we meet at *Starbucks* in Harvard Square, Cambridge. Since it was a convenient place to reach for both for us we only needed to settle on a time. We agreed on 10:00 A.M. Lorna told me that she would be wearing a brown suede jacket. I owned one also, that I would plan to wear. We would meet, for the first time on Friday the twelfth of January.

CH 2

Harvard Square to Bologna

Weeks Bridge, Harvard Square, Cambridge

That morning, I walked several blocks over ice-coated streets and arrived at Starbucks, with a few minutes still to spare. Lorna hadn't yet arrived. I picked up a newspaper and coffee and took a seat by the window so that I could watch people approaching the door while pretending to read. Lorna was exactly on time. She came in without glancing in my direction and walked directly to the counter to pick up her coffee. I was relieved to see that she was attractive. Her hair was light brown with blonde streaks. It was smooth and straight and evenly cut at collar length. She was dressed in faded blue jeans and a brown suede jacket, and as she approached my table, I saw green eyes, a nice nose, and full lips. She sat down, and we introduced ourselves.

She was an artist and she had just come from meeting with a Harvard professor whom she'd hoped would get her artwork into University publications. She set a small portfolio on the table and brushed back a lock of hair. She had made no particular effort to impress me. Her only

5

jewelry was her watch: black leather strap, large round dial with clear Arabic numerals. Black ankle socks and black, bulbous-toed workman's shoes told me that this was a serious woman.

Our conversation was about travel. I talked about France and she talked about Mexico where she had lived and gone to school for a period of time during her childhood. She had, more recently, spent a year painting in Oaxaca. That period had ended with the arrival of her daughters with whom she had then gone off to tour the archaeological sites in the area. Lorna told me that she was divorced and I told her that my wife had died a few years previously. We talked about the recent art shows we had seen while we finished our coffee. As we parted I realized that Lorna had not smiled at all during our brief meeting. It was only later that I realized that she was beautiful.

I planned to call her Sunday, but she called me first and asked if I would like to take her to a movie. I told her that I could think of nothing that would give me more pleasure. We went to a cinema that played foreign films, and watched a dark Italian comedy by the name of *Malena*. After the film I drove Lorna home and was surprised to find that she lived in Chelsea. It's a city with a bit of a gritty reputation, unlike the London borough from which it took its name.

The name, Chelsea, was derived from a similar Anglo-Saxon word that meant chalk wharf. It was used for the area on the Thames that served as the conduit for the beautiful white stone that built the city of London. Peripatetic Englishman carried the name to similar locations around the world the most famous of which is that trendy part of New York City that is home to so many world-class art galleries.

Chelsea, Massachusetts is a tiny city of more moderate size than its famous cousins. With just over two square miles it is the smallest city in the state. It occupies the only area along Boston's inner harbor that retains independent status, its neighbors, Charlestown and East Boston, having long since succumbed to Boston's growth with incorporation into the city proper.

Chelsea has had a checkered past. During the nineteenth century many factories were established, two of which, the eponymously named Chelsea Clock Company and Chelsea Tile Company, made clocks and tiles that are prized by collectors today. Less savory were the rubber and adhesive factories opened after the civil war. These industries attracted immigrants arriving from Europe and by the turn of the century Chelsea had become a crowded polyglot community. I once had a friend who learned to speak five languages in the streets while he was growing up there.

A great fire destroyed fully half of the city in 1908. Its ground level connections with Boston were severed at midcentury by construction of the Mystic River Bridge that carried northbound traffic high over the city leaving it with a certain irrelevancy that colored its politics for many years.

A major demographic change occurred in the nineteen sixties when families of the early immigrants having achieved middle class status, left for more genteel surroundings. A wave of new immigrants from Central America changed the city to Hispanic, and Spanish became the newest language of the streets. Another major fire occurred in 1973 that destroyed 18 blocks of a mostly industrial area. In 1991, Chelsea became the first city in the U.S. since the great depression to go into receivership. Boston University took over its failing schools.

I was unfamiliar with the city and Lorna directed me through its wholesale produce district, a large area of warehouses and potholed streets where eighteen-wheelers from all over the country came in with their perishables. We emerged from the market district into a warren of narrow streets and small crowded houses that gave way to a main avenue of neat redbrick townhouses. This was where Lorna had moved after her return from Mexico. I parked and she invited me in for tea.

Lorna rented out the first floor of the red brick townhouse that she owned and lived on the top two floors. A large painting of mountain scenery hung above a pier table in the foyer. The walls of the stairwell to her apartment were covered with paintings and when we reached a large book-filled hallway at the top of the stairs, I could see that the stairwell and paintings extended to the top floor. Lorna showed me into her kitchen, a large high ceiling room in the back. She used a front facing room as her studio. In the center of the kitchen was a solid Victorian worktable with heavy turned legs. We sat in drum shaped chairs covered with decorated leather that she had brought from Mexico.

Lorna had bolted to the top of one of the walls a huge cupboard that dominated the room. She had decorated it with quotations from Colette, Adrienne Rich and Duke Ellington. On other wall space she displayed ceramics that she had created: mirrors surrounded by luminous fish, plaques with botanical motifs and Spanish proverbs. Her kitchen floor was covered with a flat woven oriental carpet. On the wall behind me hung a large oil painting, a landscape of a Missouri wheat field with bold shafts of wheat in the foreground and a solitary gnarled tree in its mid ground. Lorna informed me that it had won the prestigious Boit Prize when she had been at the Museum School and had hung for a period in the Museum of Fine Arts. She lit candles and put water on for tea.

Lorna had two daughters that she loved dearly. Jeanne, her older daughter had graduated from Cornell with a degree in fine arts. She had followed it with a second degree that she had taken in nursing at Amherst. Jeanne had married Conrad, a fellow artist she had met at Cornell, and they lived in Los Angeles where Conrad had grown up. Clara, whose name Lorna never mentioned without prefacing it with "my beautiful daughter" lived nearby and was at the moment upstairs visiting. Clara had received a scholarship to study dance but had chosen instead to pursue a career in environmental sciences and was working toward her doctorate. Lorna had taken her daughters for a monthlong trip to Greece, the Greek Islands and Turkey when they were teenagers and she had spent a recent Christmas in Paris with Clara.

Clara came downstairs when the tea was ready. She was a tall and slender young woman with delicate features and large blue eyes. When she spoke, her voice rose musically, and then broke in a charming way as she moderated it. We talked about the movie we had seen, and the news of the day, and I left after telling Lorna that I would see her soon. There has never been a day since that I have not either seen Lorna or at the very least, talked with her on the phone.

We saw movies and art shows and ate at one another's houses, and engaged in all the usual activities of two people getting to know one another. Occasionally we dined out. We read the same books, subscribed to the same magazines, and we learned that we shared an addiction to PBS radio and television. If I telephoned her between 6:00 and 7:00 PM on any weekday evening, I knew that she would be listening to the Lehrer Report. Often, we compared notes on what we had read in the New Yorker, Harper's or the Atlantic Monthly. She once mentioned an art exhibit that we needed to see and I knew instantly she was referring to an interesting show that had been the focus of the previous day's discussion on PBS Radio. We met one another's friends and families became increasingly intimate, and, as we spent more time together, I realized that I loved her.

It was fun, trying to decide upon a destination for our first trip together. We chose Italy because we both loved art and especially because of a passionate interest Lorna had developed in a painter by the name of Giorgio Morandi. She had many questions about his work that she could only resolve by looking at the actual paintings. A large part of Morandi's life's work was on display in the eponymously named Morandi Museum in Bologna, and it became the focal point of our travel plans. We decided to begin our trip with a week in London because of its galleries and also, because I thought it would be a special pleasure to make love to Lorna in the particular apartment that I always rented in the Gloucester Road.

We flew on British Airways and spent a wonderful and romantic week in London. We visited the zoo and most of the important art galleries. We ate in pubs and bought scads of books that we mailed home to ourselves. We had planned to begin a month or more in Italy with a Monday morning flight to Bologna, but with growing panic I discovered my passport was missing. I thought it had probably been stolen when we had been standing in a crowd watching street musicians the previous evening. It took us nearly the entire day to replace it. We had to drag our luggage out to Heathrow, postpone our flight until evening, and then drag it all back again through the city to the American Embassy where, after some stern questioning, they issued me a new passport. It was dated September 10th, 2001.

Our flight to Bologna was two hours on a small aircraft that carried about forty passengers. Flying over Paris in the dark was romantic and I took Lorna's hand. Far below, we could see the Eiffel Tower glowing with lights and standing like a tiny jewel in the night. When we landed in Bologna, the passengers surprisingly, burst into applause. We assumed they were all Italians, and happy to be home. The night air felt soft as we emerged onto the tarmac. A bus took us to the terminal where we checked in and engaged a taxi with a helpful driver who drove us through dark, empty, arcaded streets trying to find a room. It was nearly midnight before we succeeded.

We were pleased with our room. It was large and on the second floor with a small balcony that overlooked the cobblestone street. As we climbed into the big comfortable bed, Lorna thought that she heard a horse clopping through the empty streets. I looked out and saw a young woman passing with her high heels echoing hollowly in the arcaded spaces.

In the morning we walked the half-mile to the center of town and the Morandi Museum, marveling at the faded frescos along the building line of the canopied sidewalk. We stopped at a cafe for coffee and pastries and sat at an outdoor table in the Italian air. The Bologna morning was as beautiful as we later heard the weather had been in New York City, in its final hours of innocence.

The Morandi Museum was at the end of a wide plaza in the center of town and contained a large part of the painter's life work. He has often been described as a painter's painter. John Berger called him, 'the stealthiest painter ever' perhaps because of the mystical numinosity that emanates from the objects he portrays: ordinary bottles, flowers or sometimes a view he happened upon in the street. At noon we took lunch *al fresco*, on the plaza. I sat in the sun and dozed for a couple of hours while Lorna went back to the museum for further study.

I was getting a cold and at some point I returned to our hotel to lie down. While walking back I noticed a group of men clustered around a TV set in one of the cafes. I was curious. Upon entering our room I turned on the TV just as an airliner smashed into one of the Trade Towers. A reporter was talking excitedly in Italian. Minutes later, I watched with growing apprehension as a second airliner struck the other tower. The need to talk with another person drove me to the lobby.

The hotel owner was watching the drama unfold on his TV. We stood, trading Italian superlatives until I finally had to flee to the street to find Lorna. I met her as she was walking back from the museum. I remember her look of surprise when she saw me coming toward her and her expression of innocent incomprehension as she struggled to accept the enormity of what I had to tell her.

There wasn't much news available in English and it wasn't until a few weeks had passed that our Italian was good enough to gain a fuller understanding of what had ocurred. We explored Bologna for another three days and Lorna revisited Morandi several times before we took a train for Cinque Terre, on the Italian Riviera. Here, we spent the only week of our trip that did not revolve almost entirely around art.

Cinque Terre consists of five tiny villages hanging on cliffs above the sea, that are accessible only by boat or by rail. We stayed in Manarola, the second of a line of villages that are connected by a footpath cut into the cliffs. Lorna and I walked often on the section that links Manarola with the first town which is called the *Via del Amore*—tres romantique! The longest section of the path connects to the three villages north of Manarola and it's narrow and dangerous. It rises and falls hundreds of feet between towns and there were many places that had to be traversed with care where the path had been obliterated entirely. Lorna took her sketchbook to the garden of our hotel and drew while I went off to walk the path along the cliffs. Romance has its limits.

At the end of that week we took a train to Florence where we plunged back into art. We found that books were relatively inexpensive in Italy and we loaded our luggage with wonderful art books. A week is much too short a time to spend in Florence but we were, nevertheless, able to visit most of the important churches and galleries. We climbed to the top of the Duomo, through narrow tunnels that the masons who built it in the Fifteenth Century had used during its construction. The interior of the dome depicted the end of the world with angels bearing the elect to their heavenly reward while demons dragged sinners to hell. Those saved got to keep their clothes whereas the sinners were totally naked.

From Florence we took a bus to Sienna where we stayed in a convent across from the *Cathedral of Saint Catherine of Sienna*. We became interested in the Etruscan past of the region, and we often sat and read aloud to one another at outdoor cafes, from a book written by Matthew Spender, a local sculptor, about the history of Tuscany. Our itinerary continued with sojourns in Ravenna, Padua and a brief stop in Venice. By the time we reached Milan we were reasonably fluent in Italian and able to read the local newspapers and carry on daily transactions. It was disappointing that we couldn't see the Giotti frescoes in the Scrovegni Chapel in Padua as it had been closed for restoration.

We flew home from Milan where we had spent the last few days of our trip. It was a comfortable feeling to know that unlike so many otherwise compatible couples that find travel together stressful, we had become closer at every stage of our journey.

CH 3

We decide to go to Wum

Almost as soon as we arrived home we began talking about possible destinations for our next trip. Lorna wanted to go to China; I preferred India or some island in the Mediterrean. We ruled out Spain, Austria, and Germany since Lorna didn't want to return to places she had traveled with her former husband.

Our discussions about travel found a resolution on the day that Lorna heard a radio program of charengo music on PBS radio. She fell in love with the sound of the instrument. A charengo is a kind of guitar that was once made from armadillo shells, but is today carved out of wood. It produces a unique sound and is native only to Bolivia. Lorna proposed that we fly to Bolivia, buy charengos and take lessons there. She wanted to find the unsophisticated way of life among the Indians of Bolivia that she had enjoyed in Mexico.

I agreed with her ideas and we began making preparations to head south. We outfitted ourselves at L L Bean, in Freeport, Maine and we began studying Bolivian travel guides. A trip is never certain however, until one has actual possession of the airline tickets. A couple of things intervened before our plans matured. Jeanne and Conrad bought a house on Cape Cod and moved east, and Clara fell in love.

Lorna's former husband, Joe, who lived on Cape Cod, found a wonderful piece of property in North Truro that he thought would be an ideal place for Jeanne and Conrad to own. Truro is next to Provincetown on the narrowest section of the Cape, at a place where the ocean is nearby on either side. There was a house on the property that was constructed in the old New England add-on style and it was badly in need of an update, but it was being sold at a price that was significantly below the market. Jeanne and Conrad saw its possibilities and acting quickly, bought it.

Clara had met a young man from Cameroon who had assisted her while she was struggling to load her bicycle onto a bus to Chelsea. His name was Fung and they became friends on the spot. Their friendship had progressed to the point where Clara felt it was necessary to introduce Fung to her family. Lorna invited me to a small dinner party for the introductions to take place and I brought along the wine. My only memories of Cameroon were from my stamp collecting days, but Africa had changed in fifty years and I hadn't kept up with the changes. Some national boundaries had been moved and the names of many countries had been changed. I needed to bone up on geography before I met Fung.

I found Cameroon on the map of Africa, a couple of degrees north of the equator. It was larger than I had thought: a little larger than California with a two hundred mile coastline. It was set in the corner of the Gulf of Guinea, at a point, just under the great bulge of West Africa where the coastline turned south. It was roughly triangular in shape and plunged deeply upward and into the heart of Africa, reaching as far north as Lake Chad. It shared a long border with Nigeria to the northwest and another with Chad and The Central African Republic. On the south was the Republic of the Congo, Gabon and Equatorial Guinea. Cameroon had a population of more than fifteen million people that was divided into two hundred or more ethnic groups who spoke as many languages, which is indicative of a long and complicated history. I made a list of questions about Cameroon that I would need to ask Fung.

Lorna served us steak and shrimp for dinner, the shrimp for Clara who was not eating meat at that time. I brought two bottles of the Australian Shiraz that Clara especially enjoyed. Fung impressed me immediately. He was a handsome young man with a quick sense of humor that I liked. He greeted Lorna with a quick bow and addressed her as "madam" and for me he had a firm handshake and a polite smile. Fung had been living in the United States for thirteen years and our conversation quickly turned to American politics. He seemed to be highly informed and we learned that he was studying government. Clara and he took such obvious delight in one another that we were not surprised to learn they planned to get married in the near future.

On the Cape, Jeanne and Conrad discovered that they would need to make some major renovations before they could move into their house in Truro. There were rooms that were so tiny by today's standards, that it was necessary to remove some walls. The entire house needed painting inside and out. Doors and woodwork had so many layers of old and alligatored paint that stripping to the bare wood was a necessity.

They assembled a work force of family and friends who pitched in with their work for most of the spring and early summer. My Jessie was now thirteen years old and stiff with hip dysplasia, but she, nevertheless, enjoyed coming to Truro with us and lay about in the sun while we worked nearby.

Lorna's former husband and his wife lived only twenty minutes away and could work every day. Lorna and I along with Clara and Fung spent all of our weekends there, scraping old paint and then sanding and repainting under Conrad's supervision. We never dreamed that he could be such a martinet! His approach, however, paid off, since the renovations were flawless.

People with homes in resort areas often rent them for substantial sums of money during tourist season. Jeanne and Conrad hoped that a few summer rentals would offset some of the expense of moving from California. Jeanne would look for work on the Cape. Conrad worked in the film industry and planned to commute to California for special projects from time to time. Renovations were complete by the Fourth of July. They had, by then, furnished the house with charming country furniture and antiques, several pieces of which, they had found in yard sales around the Cape. Everything ready to welcome the first guests of the season.

For almost as long as I had known her, Lorna had teased me about the contents of my basement and the closed up rooms in my house that she had never seen.

"Do you have a dead body somewhere?" she had asked a few times with what I hoped had been humor.

Continued secrecy was fast becoming an embarrassment and it was now long past the time when I should have shown her what she surely must have guessed. I finally flung open the doors of the closed up rooms so that she could see what I had concealed: hundreds of randomly filled boxes of rare items mixed with junk, and a basement that was even worse. It had been flooded by water from a freak rainstorm when seven inches of rain had fallen in a single day. The boxes that I had stored there collapsed and spilled their contents on the floor. It was too much to cope with, and I decided to leave it to the spiders. I believed that I was trapped forever. Lorna bravely insisted that was not the case, and convinced me that it was possible to deal with the mess successfully, now that we had finished in Truro.

We began by emptying the contents of my garage onto pallets that we spread around the back yard. Lorna brought along a woman to help out that she had known in Chelsea. Our next step was to empty the basement box by box, washing and cleaning, sorting and repacking, until the cellar was empty and the garage was full. At that point I found an antique dealer who looked through everything in the garage, gave me many thousands of dollars, and took everything away.

For the next six months construction and renovation became our way of life. We added two more workers from Chelsea that Lorna picked up daily and brought to Arlington and returned to Chelsea every evening. Nigel was a surprise birthday present from Lorna. She brought him rather unceremoniously to my front door on an early evening in August on a day that happened to be my birthday.

She had known Nigel for a few years. Nigel had given up a senior position in Fine Arts at the University of Liverpool to come to the U.S. with his wife and take up a position on the faculty at Boston's Museum School. Lorna consulted him frequently about her artwork. When his wife gave birth to twin girls Nigel had begun to drink very heavily and consequently, lost his job and his family. When his wife took out a court order to block him from their home he came to Lorna with nowhere to live. She couldn't let him stay with her so she brought him to my doorstep.

Nigel became a good friend and he was never any trouble. He was a hard worker and he became an important contributor to my renovations, staying with me for almost three months until he left the U.S. to return to the U.K. He had stopped drinking after a conversation in which I told him about an acquaintance of Nigel's age I once had, who, as a result of heavy drinking, needed three amputations in a year, and died six months later.

We used my basement as our center of operations. We cooked our food and ate it there or out of doors in good weather. Jessie stayed in the basement all the time now, except when I carried her to the back yard where she could use the bathroom. On good days she slept in the sun her tail wagging happily when I brought her food.

The renovations seemed to proceed according to some logic resulting from the work itself. At various times there were plumbers, electricians, or delivery trucks loaded down with supplies coming and going. There were daily trips to supply and hardware stores. Near the end, we had crews of Vietnamese floor sanders and Oriental granite workers. One day, plumbers arrived and ripped out all of my pipes. They worked throughout the house and installed a completely new plumbing system only to find out that they were at the wrong address; lucky day for me, unlucky day for the plumbers.

By February, my house had been transformed and my life with it. I was finally free of the self-imposed shackles that I had lived with for so long. Lorna and I were again ready to take up our travel plans, but we needed to wait a few more months until Clara and Fung's wedding took place at the end of March.

Fung belonged to a large family that was divided between the United States and Africa. The American branch consisted of Fung's mother along with three of his sisters who lived here with their husbands and children. Two of Fung's sisters from Cameroon were visiting with their husbands at the time of the wedding. I remember having a long conversation with one of the husbands who was a dean at the University of Yaounde. He told me that he had received his doctorate in geography from Berkeley and he talked about his doctoral research that dealt with the migrant populations of West Africa.

Fung's guests dressed in colorful African clothing and they arrived at the wedding bearing huge pots of chickens, fish, yams, fried plantains and other Cameroonian delicacies. Clara's apartment was small with three rooms apart from the kitchen, but it accommodated more than forty guests. It had space for a long line of dancers to circulate on a continuous loop when the singing and dancing began. A friend of Fung's from Mali played the *kora*. The *kora* is an elaborately strung instrument about six feet long that has a similar sound to a piano. Clara's father dragged me into the line of dancers that wove back and forth through the two rooms while we chanted, copying as best we could the folk songs that Fung's sisters were singing in the Aghem language.

Marriage in Cameroonian Society is more that a compact between two individuals. It is a joining of two extended families to form a new, larger family that imposes new rights and obligations of kinship on everyone. Every family member therefore, has a legitimate interest in the union and can address them as a part of the traditional ceremony called knock-knock or knock-door. In Wum, Fung's father had been the chief and it was important for the family to have the traditional ceremony. It took place a month later at the home of Clara's father, Joe.

Joe's next-door neighbor lent his home for the occasion and Fung's family assembled there with their friends. Clara's family gathered in her father's house. At a predetermined time a long file of Cameroonians emerged from the other house and wound their way across the intervening lawns to the door of Clara's father. They wore African dress in striking fabrics and many held brightly colored umbrellas against the light mist of the day.

The king of the Aghem people had come from Wum to attend. He wore royal fabric, dark blue heavily brocaded in orange. The king did not communicate directly with anyone, but made his wishes known only through a dignitary who accompanied him for that purpose. The Cameroon embassy in Washington, D. C. had sent an officer to serve as representative of the military. The men at the front of the line knocked on the door and Clara's father opened it. "We have heard that there is a young chicken in this house that we might acquire." the chief spokesman announced.

"Perhaps you could come in, and we can discuss it." Joe responded. Once the traditional words had been spoken, the entire group filed in. A brief wedding ceremony took place during which his majesty's spokesman made a speech expressing his majesty's sentiments. The king occupied a chair at the front of the room and was never approached directly. One approached him sideways, bent at the waist and making a silent, up and down, clapping motion of beseechment with one's hands. When the traditional celebration began however, the king joined the long line of dancers although he he was served separately and ate apart from the other guests.

Fung's father had been the king of the Aghem people, a member of the national parliament, and the head of the Protestant Church in Cameroon. Fung owned a photograph that had been taken of his father, standing beside Queen Elizabeth II and Prince Philip on the occasion of a royal visit to Cameroon. Fung's father was killed, several years ago, in a traffic accident, and the succession passed away, through the maternal line of his family. Fung however, retained the prerogatives of royalty, and Clara had become a princess.

At their wedding, Lorna and I asked about Cameroonian travel in our conversations with Fung's family. At first we were merely making small talk, but the idea gradually emerged that we might really travel there. In the days to follow, we discussed it often, and a few weeks later when the knock-door ceremony took place we had settled upon it as our next destination. Bolivia was out and Cameroon was in. It was nearly May, and Lorna and I thought that we should plan to leave for Cameroon in early January.

There was so much that we needed to learn about the country. How much money would we need? What would we do when we got there and how long would we stay? We bought every guidebook we could find and two largescale maps that showed the country in detail. We wanted to become familiar with the cities and towns that we would find there. We needed details of populations and statistics, hotels, restaurants and prices. Names of places that flow easily off our tongues today—N'Goundere, Mboucha, and Nkongsamba—were then unpronounceable. We compared prices for food and lodging in several guides, which averaged out to twenty dollars per person per day, and depending on the price of the airline tickets, we thought our trip would probably cost us about four thousand dollars each. We wanted to stay as long as we could, and this would allow us to stay four months in Cameroon. We had six months to learn what was essential to know about our new destination. We especially looked forward to seeing Wum, the principal town of the Aghem people, in the region where Fung's father had ruled.

Cameroon prides itself in its varied terrain. There are plains and grasslands, rivers and mountain ranges, and a short but beautiful coastline. Mt. Cameroon, an active volcano of 13,320 feet is the highest mountain in West Africa. Just up the coast from it, Cape Debundsha is one of the wettest places on earth, with an annual rainfall of more than four hundred inches (33 feet!).

Cameroon extends north from the rain forest of Gabon and the Congo to the Sahelian North country in the Lake Chad region. There are several large national parks, which contain almost any animal that can be found in Africa with the exception of zebras. In its advertisements designed to foster tourism, Cameroon refers to itself as Africa in miniature. Our maps showed adequate roads connecting most parts of the country. A railroad of more than five hundred miles linked the major port city of Douala with the inland capital Yaounde, and beyond to N'Goundere in the north.

Fung prepared two language guides for us, one in Aghem, and the second in the more widely-used pidgin, with useful phrases we were likely to encounter. The Aghem guide was especially useful when we got to Wum, for a few phrases from it pleased the inhabitants so much.

We studied our maps and guides constantly, familiarizing ourselves with the places we planned to visit: Douala, Yaounde, Buea, Bamenda and Bafoussam, Maroua and Garoua. We made packing lists of all the things we thought we needed to bring, but at the same time, we tried to keep everything to a minimum. Clothing took up a lot of space. We found a catalog company that sold really light travelclothing, which dried quickly and had secret security pockets. We bought water purification devices, sun block, insect repellent, a short wave radio, and small waterproof, brightly colored bags into which we could organize the contents of our backpacks. We each bought a new digital camera, and I also purchased a small portable hard drive called an image tank into which we could download our picture cards and reuse them again and again. We needed extra batteries and the means to recharge them, and adapters that would allow us to use African electrical outlets. It was November and preparations for our trip were nearly complete.

We made appointments for our inoculations in the Tropical Medicine Department at Lahey Clinic, and we were reassured by the thoroughness of the middleaged Chinese woman who was our doctor. She had travelled extensively herself and although only a yellow fever vaccination was required for entry into Cameroon, she saw to it that we had tetanus, polio, rabies and hepatitis shots as well. She prescribed enough malaria pills for a fivemonth visit, broad-spectrum antibiotics and medicine for diarrhea to take with us.

We were not allowed to apply for visas until we had purchased our airline tickets because Cameroon requires proof that those who enter the country have the means to leave it. We had a choice of SwissAir or Air France although Ethiopean Airlines was another and cheaper choice. The woman who sold us our tickets told us, "You do not want to fly on Ethiopean Airlines!" We chose Swiss Air because Fung's relatives had told us not to fly on Air France because our luggage would be lost. I remembered Air France had once left my luggage in Paris when I had flown to Bordeaux.

We sent off proof of ticket purchases along with our visa requests to the Cameroonian embassy in Washington and received our passports back, stamped for three-month visits, just before Christmas. There were less than two weeks remaining before our departure. Our bags were packed and we were ready to go.

CH 4

First days in Cameroon

We flew out of Boston in the middle of January on one of the coldest nights in a year of extreme cold. Before we left, Clara gave us a family tree that she had drawn up with the names of Fung's brothers and sisters, the people they were married to and their children, ten families in all. The first part of our flight was the usual transoceanic eight-hour ordeal in cramped seats. Morning came early, and there was a two-hour stopover in Zurich before we embarked on our flight south to Douala. We were scheduled to arrive in Douala in the early evening.

From forty thousand feet, the Mediterranean coast of France looked like a huge map. We were too high to see anything other than the large geographical aspects of the landscape below. Our flight path was well to the west of Corsica and Sardinia, which were visible only as huge cloudbanks halfway to the horizon. The coast of Africa appeared clear and sharply defined, and then I guessed we were over Algeria.

All of North Africa was covered with a thin haze called the harmattan, a dust-laden wind from the Sahara mixed with wood smoke from cooking in the region. It created a haze that filtered the sunlight. We flew for some hours, as the color of the earth below changed slowly, from the earth tones of the Sahara, to the pale greens of the Nigerian grasslands. Then we were over ocean again and beginning to descend to our first and only stop, which was Malabo, the island capital of Equatorial Guinea. As we lost altitude, the haze occasionally cleared enough to see oil platforms and a few small boats in the waters around the island. Our captain began a series of landing announcements. Speaking first in German, then in French and English, he told those of us who were continuing on to Douala to remain on the plane. He warned us also, that pictures of the airport in Malabo were strictly forbidden.

We had read that there was a very beautiful mountain on the island, a volcano with an altitude of more than 3100 meters (13,000 feet). The haze was so deep, however that we couldn't see beyond the wall of the forest surrounding the airport. There was a single landing strip bordered by a wide swath of grass with a square paved area to the side, on which were parked a dozen or so propeller driven airliners and one very large bizarre looking jet craft that seemed designed for moving massive equipment. That was all we were able to see of Equatorial Guinea, one of Africa's most vicious dictatorships. Our flight resumed after about an hour. Two thirds of the passengers, presumably oil field workers, had disembarked at Malabo, and we luxuriated in the new spaciousness of our surroundings.

The sun was beginning to set as we approached Cameroon, and the sky was suffused with a wondrous mauve light. We flew at a lower altitude on the short flight to Douala, and the clouds below us resembled a field of fleece. To the northeast, there was an immense pile of clouds, curiously flat topped, which emerged from the cloud plain and rose, perhaps, another ten thousand feet. We assumed that it obscured Mt. Cameroon, the 4090-meter volcano that was the highest peak in West Africa. We came in over the coastal town of Limbe, flying over massive plantations with lines of regularly planted trees.

Dusk had fallen by the time we reached Douala. Stepping into the tropical evening of the mostly empty airport seemed like a warm August evening at home. Two long, empty corridors took us to the counter where our visas and immigration cards were checked allowing us to pass into a large hall where the baggage came onto the carousel.

We immediately saw Elsa and Nia, Fung's brother and sister. Elsa, whom we had previously met at Clara's wedding, was short and slightly plump with a round face and glasses while Nia was formidable looking in the red, green and yellow of the national football (soccer) team. He wore a red baseball cap and leaned slightly back as he stood to counterbalance the weight of his powerful chest and stomach. We also met John, their driver, who helped us to transfer our baggage to their pickup truck, parked nearby.

Perhaps because we were tired, we felt relaxed and comfortable. Nia and John carefully lashed our baggage to the bed of the truck, while a group of young boys gathered around asking pesty questions to distract us from seeing the actions of their companions who were trying determinably, to steal something. *'Va t'en.'* and *'Ficher le camp.'* we shouted, using out French slang for "scram' as we shooed them away. Nia warned us that the Bonaberi Bridge that crossed the Wouri River was a particularly dangerous place for thefts and he tied our luggage extra securely to the bed of the truck.

Elsa was dissatisfied with the hotel we had planned to use. She thought that Douala was an unsuitable place for us to stay, because of mosquitos and the possibility of crime in the area. She planned instead to take us to a hotel in Buea, forty miles from Douala, and high enough above sea level to be mosquito-free. Fung's family clearly felt a heavy responsibility for our safety.

Night had fallen by the time we left the airport. Although we were in a big city, traffic moved in a chaotic fashion without the assistance of either policemen or traffic signals. We stopped for bottled water on a main street in the city at a store named Zepol's, a wonderful bakery established by Greeks about forty years previously. It was a large store with a score of glass cases filled with tempting bakery items, desserts and readymade sandwiches. It also had a large area for groceries. We didn't realize at the time what a unique establishment it was for we never saw a similar store in all of Cameroon.

We left the main part of the city and crossed the bridge on the Wouri River into Bonaberi without incident, in spite of the dire predictions made to us when we were loading. We made a stop to visit Fung's aunt Cecelia at a place just off the main road. A long wall ran the length of her street, with gates for each residence. We stopped at her gate and rang her on the intercom. Aunt Cecelia came down to meet us and we chatted for a few minutes, but passed on her invitation to come in because it was getting late and we still had a distance to travel.

We continued for several miles through an industrial area that was open and uncluttered. Most of the buildings we passed were in darkness and were well set back from the road that roughly paralleled the coast. We saw large filling stations where trucks were fueling, and we passed several neonlighted clubs, filled with seated drinkers, silhouetted in dim light. We had to stop at a toll station manned by a few soldiers at a roadside shack. After we paid our toll, they removed a nail-studded strip from the roadway, allowing us to pass.

We entered onto a long, straight, dark road that cut through palm plantations for several miles. We had seen this part of the coast from our plane during the landing approach. Several miles farther, the road began to gradually rise above the plain and at an area of small shops and bars called Mutungene, we turned sharply inland. For the next ten or twelve miles, the road rose and fell, but overall, we were going higher. Houses and shops were scattered along the road, interspersed with dark wooded areas. It was now nearly 10:00 PM, but there were still many people walking along the edge of the road, even in places where there were no signs of habitation.

The warm, humid evening had turned dry and cooler. Small tradesmen at makeshift stands were still selling their wares by lantern light. There was another toll station, and then we passed through a large motor park that was assembled around a traffic circle where dozens of tiny bus lines had their offices. Most of the 'buses were actually garishly painted modified vans.

We had come nearly 45 miles from Douala and risen about 3,000 feet. As the road continued gradually upward, there was little sense of altitude, and it was hard to believe that we were on a massive mountain. Eventually we turned into a large courtyard, which had a half dozen umbrella-tables spread about. There was a low cement building with a restaurant at the front and two floors of rooms to the rear. This was our hotel, and it was called the OIC Pavilion. It was not unlike many motels we had seen in the U.S. Our room was large, and overlooked an acre or so of makeshift tables shaded by rusted metal roofing. There were iron security grills over the windows, but there were no screens, and the walls, ceiling and floor were made of concrete. The furniture was old fashioned but adequate. The bathroom had a working shower. Nia and John helped us with our luggage, and since the hour was late everyone was eager to leave. Elsa promised to come back in the morning to help us change our currency and plan our visit.

Next morning, we took our breakfast on a small porch connected to the dining room at the front of the hotel: orange juice, a plain omelet, bread and coffee. We watched the traffic along the road that we had arrived on. The road was wide enough for two lines of traffic in each direction and traffic was heavy. Taxis were stopping everywhere to pick up or discharge passengers. Seven or eight out of every ten vehicles on the road were yellow *share taxis*, whose passengers shared rides for trips within the town. Each trip was called a drop. The fare was 150 Central African Francs (about 30 cents U.S.) for each person to travel any distance within town limits. This was the road that was under construction when Mary Kingsley had written her nineteenth century book, *Travels in West Africa*. She wrote that it was the most magnificent road in West Africa. It terminated a mile and a half beyond our hotel at a place where the mountain began to rise sharply to its 13, 760' cone, now hidden from view by the haze.

Nia and Elsa arrived shortly after breakfast. They wanted to take us sightseeing, but first we needed to exchange our U.S. dollars for local currency. Cameroon, along with four other African countries, uses the Central African franc (CFA). We hired their taxi driver for the entire day, and drove first to the Office of the Church Treasurer to exchange our money. The church offices were about a mile away, occupying a large campus, behind which the main mass of the mountain rose steeply into the mist. Church dignitaries lived on the highest part of the campus with the church offices below.

We drove up a steep incline and were waved through an iron gate by a uniformed guard who occupied a tiny guardhouse. Profusions of tall palm trees landscaped the campus, among which banana trees grew like weeds. The Treasurer's Office opened onto the central garden of a cloister. We were introduced to the chief financial officer, who exchanged most of our money for CFAs. I held back ten one hundred dollar bills, which I slid into a secret pocket. Elsa took charge of our money for safekeeping, and dispensed the equivalent of a thousand dollars to each of us for our immediate expenses.

When we were planning our trip, the exchange rate had stood at 657 CFAs per dollar, but the American dollar had been losing value against other currencies for more than a year, and we received only 540 CFAs per dollar. The money came in ten—and twenty-thousand CFA notes, and Elsa showed us how to arrange them in packets, folding every fifth or tenth note over the others and then folding once more the resulting group of bills.

Although the sun was shining brightly, and the temperature was comfortable, the mountain was still hidden in the clouds. In the hundred and ten years since Mary Kingsley had been here the main Buea road had filled up with small businesses. Buildings, consisting of cement blocks or precast concrete, with rusting or bent corrugated metal roofs, had sprung up along the road. There were lines of small cell-like stores with homemade signs and found materials for doors that gave them a provisional or *ad hoc* appearance. One could find a tire repair shop or a furniture maker next door to an undertaker or a bar.

Grocery stores sold bottled water and a few imported canned goods, toiletries and cosmetics. Most stores would have only as much stock as people in the U.S. keep on their pantry shelves. Dairy was nonexistent, except in boulangeries, where butter and cheese imported from Europe were available. Cold beer was plentiful and sold predominantly in bars. Fresh food was usually found in large outdoor markets or at tiny stalls or individual stands along the streets.

We stopped at a banana stand and bought a large hand for 200 CFAs to keep our hunger at bay until lunch. We drove along the coastal road through miles of plantations to a massive hill of black volcanic ash that came down to the road only yards from the sea. The flowing lava had reached this point during the last eruption of Mt. Cameroon in 1999. We scrambled a few hundred feet up the flow and took turns assuming intrepid poses for photos. Back on the road, we were besieged by souvenir vendors and bought some pictures of the eruption in progress.

With occasional glimpses of the ocean, we drove back along the coastal road into Limbe. Nia lived in Limbe, which had been called

Victoria during the British proctectorate period following WWI. We stopped for lunch at a place called the Fish Shack by the shore. It was a fairly large restaurant that consisted of a half dozen large gazebos with grass roofs shading the tables where we ate. Our driver joined us as we placed our orders for beer and fish from the nearby kitchen.

The fish was whole barracuda, each more than a foot long, which was served to us on large platters. There were no utensils, requiring us to eat with our fingers. I found that difficult because the cooked fish broke up so easily, but I had more success after I pressed the backbone into service as a tool. The fish was absolutely fresh, moist and delicious. We sat at different tables, and Nia, who shared a table with Lorna, asked if he could have the head that she was not going to eat. He told her it was the best part of the fish. Lorna, however, wanted to make a drawing of it, and she wouldn't let him have it.

We visited Cynthia and Pastor's house that evening, along with Elsa and her husband Paul, who brought us there in their Toyota 4x4. Pastor was the head of the Protestant Church in Cameroon and was known by the title of Moderator. The head of the church's house was behind the Church office. Fung's father had been the previous Church Moderator, and his children, including Fung, had grown up there. We sipped some excellent Bordeaux, but stayed a little less than an hour. As new members of Fung's family, our visit was a required formality.

Later that evening, we sat with Paul and Elsa at one of the umbrella tables at the front of our hotel and drank some beer. Cameroon makes excellent beer. In the most remote village, far from major roads, one encounters the huge red "33" (Trente-tois) trucks or yellow Castel trucks with their loads of beer. Refrigeration is possible because power lines extend to most parts of the country, making cold beer always available. The beer is sold in .67 liter bottles that seemed to be almost as big as our quart bottles.

Lorna and I liked Paul immensely. He had a rich baritone voice and a blacker skin than most other Cameroonians we had met. Color didn't seem to be a sensitive subject for people in Cameroon, and Paul, I believe, would have been less handsome had he been of lighter color. We talked about our plans and itinerary. Elsa thought we should leave soon if we wanted to visit the far north because temperatures there were still relatively moderate. If we waited, temperatures would exceed 100 degrees. Fung's brother Nia could take some time off and he would accompany us for security. When Paul and Elsa left us that evening, they invited us to their home for dinner the following evening.

The next day was Saturday and we awoke to a sound like an angry beehive that was becoming louder and angrier by the minute. We looked out of our window and saw that the acres of stalls below were swarming with people who were pouring in from the road and jamming every aisle. We were all out of toothpaste and soap, none of which the hotel supplied, so after breakfast I went over to the market to shop. Every stall was filled, and excess vendors lined the street along the fence at the front of our hotel. The road was jammed with taxis and I wanted to take a photograph of the traffic, but as soon as I took my camera out, people along the fence, fearing that I might photograph them, angrily assailed me. I quickly put it way, but the hard looks still coming my way were slow to dissolve.

Vendors were arranged by categories in the market. Three aisles were the devoted to clothing with many fabric dealers and nearby tailors who could fashion their cloth into anything one might desire. Grains and dried beans shared a special location near the entrance. Fresh fruits and vegetables took up a large area. I found a section that contained medications that could only be obtained through prescriptions in most other countries. I checked their expiration dates and was surprised to see that they were all current. Much of what was sold at the market came from Nigeria.

Cameroon, like Canada, has two official languages, French and English. We were, however, in one of the two provinces where English predominated as a result of a 1961 plebiscite that chose to associate with French speaking Cameroon rather than English speaking Nigeria. I visited the butcher's stalls along the rear of the market and found that the butchers spoke only in French. I had worked part-time as a meatcutter when I was in college and I told the butchers, in French, that I too had been a butcher. They were curious and assumed that I had worked in Paris, and it surprised them them to learn that I was an American from Boston.

The butchers sold only beef. If one wanted chicken or goat, it was necessary to buy it alive and kill it oneself. Their beef was very lean and small. A porterhouse steak was about the size of an American pork chop. Four legs of a recently slaughtered animal were still on display, but the head had already been sold. One butcher, who seemed to be in charge, proudly showed off a neat braid he had made from the large intestine. Everything was covered with flies. Before I moved on, I watched a woman, cradling a baby, bargain for the huge, hairy and fatty lump of flesh from behind the neck of the animal.

I came to a poultry section, where chickens were confined in large soft round baskets, each basket containing ten chickens or more. Two sides of the basket were lashed together leaving a small space through which some of the chickens could poke their heads out. Lorna loves chickens, and I wanted to show her the way they were confined in the market. When I went back to our hotel room, she was busy drawing the barracuda head that she had saved from our previous day's lunch. By the time she finished her drawing and we got back to the market, the chickens had been turned loose.

That evening, Paul came with his car, a two-year old Toyota stationwagon, to bring us to dinner at his house. As we drove there, his radio was playing the country classic with the lyrics:

> *You picked a fine time to leave me Lucille—*
> *Four hungry children and the crops in the field.*
> *You picked a fine time to leave me Lucille!*

Paul and Elsa's house was similar to, but not as large as, the Moderator's house. We met their sons, Luke and Matthew, young men of college age. Paul opened a bottle of French wine to accompany a delicious meal of chicken and vegetables. We had never tasted huckleberry greens, known in Cameroon as *jama jama*. It resembled chopped spinach with a similar taste, perhaps more bitter, but with a paler, very intense green color.

After dinner we attended the dress rehearsal for a choral concert. It was a celebration for the twenty-fifth anniversary of the first choir established on the north side of the Mungo River, the linguistic boundary between the French and English speaking parts of the country which we had crossed unnoticed, as we drove to Buea from Douala on the night we arrived.

The choir filled all the seats of a large auditorium. It was made up almost entirely of women in white dresses with the exception of a few men who took turns as directors and sat along the side of the hall. The audience, all twelve of us, sat onstage in a line of chairs that faced the singers. The Governor of the province sat with his assistant to our left, with Elsa and Paul to our right. Although we were unfamiliar with the music, we found the rich harmonies of the accappella voices extremely engaging. Elsa and Paul were highly musically literate and took their music very seriously. We have seldom enjoyed choral music more.

The next day was a Sunday. We were having our breakfast on the porch of the hotel when a thin man of medium height, wearing a suit too large for him, placed his business card on our table and took a seat. He told us that he worked for the development company that had built our hotel, but what he wanted to talk about was religion. He proudly informed us that he was soon to be ordained as a Pentecostal minister. Actually he was hungry and wanted us to buy his breakfast, which we did. He talked about his life. He told us his pay was a hundred and forty CFAS a month—good pay in Cameroon. However, he had two wives and four children, and AIDS, or 'SIDA' as it is called in French. The cost of his medication left him with little money to support his family.

He was still sitting with us when Luke, Elsa and Paul's older son, arrived. Luke looked very nice in a white shirt, tie, and sport jacket. He was there, he informed us, to drive us to church. The church was nearby, and occupied a small hill at the end of a street off the main road. It was a modern building with lots of brick and polished wood, with a high slanted asymmetric roof and a separate, freestanding bell tower in front. The churchgoers were well dressed. Most of the men wore business suits, while the women dressed in brightly colored wraparounds and headscarves. I stood in the doorway chatting with Luke, while Lorna sat inside with Elsa. The service lasted three hours, a long time, but for the parishioners it was as much an entertainment as a duty, and they came out in high spirits, gathering into lingering groups for conversations from which much laughter emerged.

CH 5

Train to the far north

We decided to leave for the North the first thing Monday morning, and we spent the rest of Sunday preparing for our trip. We carried light travel packs and left whatever we thought might be redundant at Elsa's house. She telephoned us around sundown to tell us that the mists had lifted enough for us to see the mountain. We went outside to look and discerned its faint outline.

When Nia knocked on our door in the morning we were ready to leave. Elsa had banked our money with the treasurer at the church office and withdrew a million CFAs (2,000 dollars) for our use on the trip north. She gave Nia enough CFAs to cover taxi, bus and train fares. Nia had taken two weeks of uncompensated leave from his job as a printer in Limbe to come with us. He had never been to the north but he had heard the same stories that we had all heard about the dangers that existed there and he felt responsible for our safety. We agreed to pay him sixty dollars a week as compensation for his loss of pay. He had arranged for a friend who owned a taxi to take us to Douala, where we could find a bus that went to Yaounde.

We joined a stream of traffic consisting mostly of sharetaxis heading down the long grade toward the coastal road ten miles away. The road to the coast was not all downhill but rose in many places. There was not a sense of coming off a huge mountain because visibility at that time of year was so limited, and neither the mountain above nor the coast beyond, were visible.

It took us nearly an hour to reach Douala. At closer and closer intervals as we approached the city, we saw the remains of every vehicle that had ever been wrecked there, rusting into various stages of oxidation. There was a large motor park at Bonaberi just before the bridge into the city where hordes of cyclists waited on their light Japanese motorcycles to take people across the bridge to their jobs.

The park also accommodated scores of transport agencies that carried people between cities in four—or five-seat window vans. They were gaudily painted and covered with the logos of their operators. They would leave only when they had been filled with customers, however long that might be. Along with people there was much merchandise shipped also. Piled on the roofs were large bags of yams, sacks of grain, stalks of bananas, and quite often, live goats as well as the passenger's luggage. Taxis were everywhere, discharging or picking up passengers, and mixed with the crowds were vendors, both those with permanent stalls and those who strolled with their inventories on their heads.

We didn't stop there, but we drove directly into the city where we could find large comfortable buses similar to those one takes for long trips in the U.S. We found Douala, being at sealevel, noticeably warmer than Buea. It was like a very hot summer day at home. The intercity bus station was in an area of streets with ruined pavements, tucked behind the main business district of stores, restaurants and large hotels.

Nia held us together in a tight group as we boarded the bus, and he always positioned himself in a way that he would be able to protect us if an assault occurred. Our bus was comfortable and the trip to Yaounde took four hours along a well-paved two-lane highway with light traffic. Several huge lumber trucks passed us, each of which carried three massive logs of mahogany or padouk secured with chains to the flatbed. We saw few towns or houses along the road except at a place named Edea where there was a large aluminum plant that made the corrugated roofing that had largely replaced grass roofs around the country.

Yaounde was an attractive city with with green hills, trees, and wide avenues. Its bus station was on the outskirts of the city. The bus turned down a narrow ramp into a small yard where we disembarked. We retrieved our packs from the roof of the bus and, walking closely together for safety, made our way back up the ramp to the entrance where several taxis had congregated. Nia selected the newest looking vehicle, and rejected several drivers who had aggressively tried to lure us into their more suspect looking vehicles.

We had planned to visit the American Embassy but when we got there we found it was closed for Martin Luther King's Day. Nia was carrying a heavy bag of supplies that we had brought from America to deliver to his sister Susan who lived in Yaounde with her husband, a dean at the university. We had met them previously at Clara's wedding. They lived on one of the scores of residential hills surrounding the city. There were imposing public buildings, and the residential streets were attractive but unpaved and often steep. Our cab raised clouds of red dust and bottomed out frequently as the driver, following Nia's directions, took a confusing sequence of left and right turns over deeply rutted streets.

Susan and Mark lived in a cool and comfortable looking stone ranch landscaped with ornamental plants of varieties that would be grown indoors, in Boston. Their Volvo station wagon was in the driveway, but they were away for a few days. Their family servants greeted us and offered to produce a meal but we demurred. We delivered the bag we had brought from America and got back into our waiting taxi.

We decided to go to the railroad station first and find out about the train schedules, but we were hungry. Our driver recommended a restaurant called "La Feuille Verte" (the green leaf, where the four of us, driver included, lunched together on fish, rice and beer.

When we arrived at the train station we found that the train would leave that evening at 6:30 PM, and that there would not be another for two days. Tickets went on sale at 5; 00 P.M. Pastor had arranged rooms for us at the Protestant Center that we would not need if we left that evening. We decided to use them anyway and rest until train time. We asked our driver to come back for us at 4:30 P.M. I was worried about it, but he was on time, and on the way to the station we stopped at a patisserie where we bought bread, cheese, and water to sustain us for the fourteen or fifteen hours we expected to be on the train.

The train station was set back and low, about a hundred yards from the avenue. Taxis were parked at all angles in the large space in front of it. There was a long line of stalls with their backs to the avenue that sold food and sundries for travelers. Nia warned us that train stations were especially dangerous places as he paid our taxi driver and led us into the station.

It was crowded but we found a free place to stand while Nia brought our passports to the guichet to purchase our tickets. Foreigners must show their passports in order to travel. While he was away, we saw a wretched creature, barely recognizable as human, dragging himself around the ankles of the crowd. He saw us and scuttled in our direction waving a claw-like hand. I had a small coin that I gave him and he crawled away from us. When the gate opened we were picked up by the press of the crowd and carried in a sudden rush that brought us out to the platform where we were set free.

We located our train car and found the seats whose numbers matched our tickets. Our car had rows of alternately facing seats with space for luggage overhead. Many family groups with children occupied pairs of seats. Nia and Lorna took facing seats and I sat next to Lorna on the aisle. I faced an empty seat, but a moment later, a very beautiful woman came in and took it. She was slender and graceful with delicate features and a smooth coffee colored complexion. She was dressed in African style, a blue wrap-around decorated with the yellow insignia of the bank she worked for.

She left her purse on the seat while she left the train. She returned only when it was nearly time to leave, making our hyper-vigilance about our possessions feel a little silly. She settled demurely into her seat, eyes modestly downcast and fingers laced together. The train left, and at some point she fell asleep. But before closing her eyes, she took a small slip of lace and wound it around her hands to secure them while she slept. How elegant, I thought. Nia had dismissed her after trying to ask her something in English to which she did not respond, or give any indication that she understood. A few hours later at a train stop she bought a bag of vine wrapped, rolled banana leaves called "batons" from a vendor who was loudly shouting, "baton, baton, baton!"

I was curious about them, and asked her in French what they were used for. She politely explained to me that they contained pounded, fermented Mangos that were used to make a drink. As the night went on we snacked on our cheese and bread but I found it impossible to sleep on the train. At 2:30 AM it was 8:30 PM in Boston and still the previous evening. I telephoned my sister on my cellphone, and was as surprised as she was when she answered. She was excited to hear from us and had been trying to follow our progress on a map of Africa. I gave her the name of our last train stop. I also called an old school friend and his wife with whom Lorna and I had spent the previous New Years Eve. They found it hard to believe that I was calling from the interior of Africa, since the call had come in to them as if it had been from the next town.

At every train stop during the night there were vendors with loads on their heads moving about on the dark platforms. They made their small livings by selling oranges they had peeled or pineapples they had trimmed or by finding some other way to add value to something people would buy. A large group of soldiers boarded the train in the morning. They were stationed in the north, we heard, to prevent train robberies which were previously rampant in that part of the country.

The train line ended in N'Gaoundere, the Capitol of Adamawa Province. It was a city surrounded by a circle of mountains high enough to ward off most of the eye watering smoke caused by the burning on the plains that prepared the land for the new planting season. N'Gaoundere's population of 45,000 was substantial, but it was thinly spread over a wide area. The business section was three miles from the railroad station. North Cameroon begins here and extends to Lake Chad through the two most northern provinces, called Nord and Extreme Nord. Moslems predominate in these areas and we saw many Mosques. There is a sizeable Christian community here also, but the two religions seem to coexist in an atmosphere of mutual respect. Motor vehicles are rare in this part of the country and most transport is by motorcycle.

We engaged three motorcycles at the railroad station to take us to the Hotel du Rail, which was about a half mile away. Our guidebook had recommended staying there, with the caveat that it had cockroaches as large as birds. To Lorna's disappointment, that was untrue, at least during our visit. For our trip to Africa, Lorna had prepared about twenty pounds of paper for drawing by coating each sheet with a gesso wash, but for our trip north, she only carried along enough to make two books of drawings. She began them at N'Gaoundere with a series of sketches of the palm trees surrounding the Hotel du Rail.

We decided to postpone any sightseeing in N'Gaoundere until our return trip and we took a bus early next morning for Garoua, 180 miles to the north. The bus station was next to the train station and the bus we chose was a large window van, its roof piled high with goods being shipped to Garoua.

I carried my camera in a black string bag and I began taking pictures from the bus as soon as we left the station, although I sneaked some pictures at the station when nobody seemed to be paying attention. I was careful because I had upset people whenever I hadn't gotten permission to take their pictures.

CH 6

N'Gaoundere to Garoua

As we came down from the mountains surrounding N'Gaoundere, we passed a line of Fulani cattle, great beasts with large humps at their necks and long curved horns. They were walking in the road with their Fulani minder, who never glanced in our direction as we passed. We entered onto a narrow highway that crossed a wide plain with a fringe of distant hills barely visible through the smoke of the fires on the land.

As soon as we left N'Gaoundere, we began to see the characteristic dwellings of the area, room-sized structures with conical grass roofs. They were constructed of sundried bricks in the beautiful earth tones of the local soils. They occurred sometimes singly, but often assembled into groups, compounds, or even villages. The walls of the houses were often extended to form private enclosures, and fences made with bundles of straw or woven mats were often added. Natural materials were used in every aspect of life. There were few chickens, but small goats wandered everywhere, a pygmy variety common to the north. We saw children sitting in groups under trees for their schooling, and women wearing blouses and wrap-around skirts, bent low, working in the fields or walking on the sides of the road with heavy burdens on their heads. The men dressed in shirts and trousers and sat together talking or napping in the shade.

We sat, three across, on the bus; I was behind the driver and took pictures of the changing scenery. It was a hot and dry landscape. The road crossed empty riverbeds, where people were at work digging deep holes to find water. Single crops predominated. One region would have large fields of millet, and then we would pass into another area where there were artesian wells, and onions predominated. Cotton was a common crop. It was planted randomly rather than in neat rows. We often, saw bales of cotton that had been left on the side of the road for pick up and shipment to Nigeria that manufactured most of the cloth sold in Cameroon.

The road was broken up in many places and our driver often veered onto the dirt for smoother driving. A few times we passed huge overladen trucks that had stalled beside the road, and were leaning precariously from flat tires or broken axles. Our driver always stopped to offer them water. We frequently passed eight-foot tall termite mounds as we wound through low hills thinly scattered with trees.

We passed through a few small villages with business districts, which seemed to have been created from what looked like a line of concrete modular cellblocks that had been dropped at the edge of the road and used by local people to set up businesses. A power line followed the road and cold drinks were always available. We were stopped by a military checkpoint on the outskirts of Garoua where we were asked to show our papers. I had left the yellow card that recorded my yellow fever immunization in Buea, and the officer had asked to see it with my passport. Nia told him that I was his relative, and the officer looked demonstrably from Nia to me several times, which greatly entertained the soldiers that accompanied him. They were very good humored and waved to us enthusiastically as we went on our way.

Cameroon has four seaports. Douala, Limbe and Kribi are on the coast, and the fourth, Garoua, is a thousand miles inland. It is only usable seasonally and depends on the rainy season and a release of water from nearby Lake Lagdo. It is on the Benue River, which is dry half the year, but connects to the Niger River, which in turn, connects it to the sea. Crossing the bridge into the city we saw that there were only stagnant bowls of water left in its bed.

We drove immediately onto a broad avenue with a center strip. There were few trees and the city had a sun-bleached feel. We passed a Mosque and a few blocks of stores before we turned into the street where the bus station was located. We collected our backpacks from the roof of the bus and engaged three motorcycles to take us to the Hiala Inn, our guidebook's recommendation. A large courtyard where the office was located formed a hub from which a restaurant and two lines of rooms branched. Decorative cactus landscaped the entire Inn. Rooms, walls, and restaurant were covered with smooth pinkish-colored stucco. Small lizards four to six inches long darted about the walls and even came inside our rooms having squeezed through the spaces around our air conditioner.

Nia was not happy with the room that he was given, and we had to pay extra for one that satisfied him. It was nearly two o'clock by the time we had stored our bags and eaten lunch. Our map of Garoua indicated a handicraft complex near the city center and we decided to visit it that afternoon. We hired three motorcycle taxis and we were off. At the center Lorna found some beads that she liked for her daughters. They were made from dime-sized disks cut from ostrich eggs, which had then been dyed red and strung together like rolls of coins. We enjoyed the walk back to our hotel, stopping several times to chat with shopkeepers sitting in front of their places of business.

I wanted to take some pictures when we got back and unpacked to find my camera. I couldn't find it anywhere and my first thought was that it had been stolen. I couldn't imagine how that could have occurred, since my baggage had been either under my control or under lock and key since we left the bus. The loss of my camera was depressing, but the thought occurred to me that perhaps I had left it on the bus. I did not share this thought with either Nia or Lorna.

The next morning, without saying anything further, I walked to the ticket office and asked the young man in charge if my camera had been turned in. Since we were in a Francophone section of Cameroon, I had to conduct my business in French. "On ne le trouve pas" he responded, 'they hadn't found it'. I described the camera and its bag and I offered a reward for its recovery. The young man asked me to wait while he telephoned Maroua, to which our bus had continued after we had gotten off.

When he hung up he told me that my camera had been found and was being sent back to Garoua on the next bus. If I could return at "quatorze heures" (two o'clock) he would have it for me. Nia and Lorna were amazed at my good fortune and that afternoon they accompanied me back to the bus station to await the arrival of my peripatetic camera. We passed time by chatting with the vendors who gathered at the bus stop, all of whom were women. Their brightly colored costumes were a vivid contrast with the earth tones of their surroundings. A woman dressed in a blue and green print squatted over a basket of smoked fish. She had tucked their tails into their mouths, making quoits, before she smoked them.

"Capitaine fume?" I asked her. Capitaine is the name used locally for the Nile Perch that we were usually served when we ordered fish. She smiled as she nodded that I was correct and offered them to me for a hundred CFAs apiece (twenty cents). We bought large ripe mangos for the same price and dripped the juice all over ourselves as we consumed them. There was no place to clean up and we had to use the bathroom before the bus showed up. It was a cement room with a hole in the floor. Two hours later, my traveling camera arrived. At Nia's suggestion I tipped the young man who had made the call, 20,000 CFAS, the equivalent of forty dollars. I later found out that I had given him more than many Cameroonians can earn in a month.

We crossed several busy streets on the way back to our hotel. I was still basking happily in the pleasure of my good luck when Nia told me sharply, to take my hands out of my pockets. It was an order! "What if you had to move fast?" he asked as if I was a schoolboy that he was admonishing. I was holding onto my camera to reassure myself that it was really back in my pocket, and I complied as slowly and with about as much surliness, as I was capable of showing.

Lorna wanted to work on her sketchbook when we got back to our hotel and she thought that a lizard might make an interesting study. There were dozens of them on the walls surrounding the courtyard but plantings made them hard to reach. Across the street, however, we saw a wall that ran back from the street along a driveway that separated a security agency from an abandoned cinema next door. It was eight feet high, and constructed of pebbly stucco, covered in moss, and badly deteriorating, which created scores of nooks and crannies for the little creatures to live.

Lorna took out her collection jar, and we began the chase. The little creatures moved so fast that we weren't able to catch one. Two uniformed security officers standing on porch of the agency were watching us with frank curiousity. One of them, a balding middle-aged man with sergeant's stripes on his sleeve, finally strolled over to find out what we were doing. He spoke French and Lorna addressed him in a mixture of French from school and Spanish, in which she is fluent. When he was still puzzled, I tried my French. I told him that Lorna was an artist and that we were trying to catch a lizard for her to draw. This elicited an immediate smile. He was himself an artist, he informed us as he zealously joined the chase.

The other guard, who was a young woman, watched skeptically from the porch. We attracted the attention of a group of passing boys who joined in eagerly when they found out what was happening. Our group was growing. More security guards had come out and joined in and Nia had come across the street. He thought it might help if we offered a reward and suggested 1000 CFAs (about two dollars) would be suitable. There were now about fifteen or more people climbing around the wall, and they were all spurred on by the prospect of money. A young guard who was quicker than anyone else finally ended the hunt successfully when he brought Lorna a fat little lizard he had caught between thumb and forefinger. Nia told us that afterwards, many of the people assembled, expressed questions about who we were and where we had come from. There had been a lively discussion and the consensus was that we were Spaniards even after he had tried to tell them otherwise.

Nia arranged a trip to a market for the next day. There was a market in the north part of Garoua that I thought we could visit for the small price of three motorcycle trips in each direction, but instead he hired a taxi to take us to a large regional market in Guider, fifty miles away and almost halfway to Maroua, our next major stop.

The road was heavily potholed and our driver, a slender quiet man by the name of Gabrila, drove at top speed. His laid back manner was at odds with his exuberant driving style. We swerved into the dirt to avoid holes so often that it seemed that most of our trip was off-road. For many miles before we reached Guider, we passed people carrying large loads on their heads or pulling heavily laden carts in the same direction that we were headed.

When we arrived, we parked in an area where car parts were sold and wandered through the market in a group. There was an enormous amount of food for sale—sacks of various grains, beans, cocoyams, and baskets of dark green huckleberry that is boiled like spinach to make Jama Jama. There was a section where Nigerians sold colorful bolts of fabric, in striking designs that women used in their garments. Their clothing was often emblazoned with particular insignia like the green Protestant cloth or a brown cloth that had pictures of Ange Patasse, the president of the Central African Republic. Many men wore caftans and long Moslem robes, but Gabrila informed me that clothing was usually a matter of preference rather than religion.

Several people were grilling meat in one shady corner of the market, and nearby, we found some logs and stumps to sit on and had lunch. I had had a dull ache in my jaw all morning, but it was no longer dull. I was in intense pain. It seemed to originate in my left temple, radiate across my left eye socket and then down and back along my lower jaw. It was like nothing I had ever felt before. I thought that it was probably neuralgia and I told Lorna and Nia about it. We asked around and found that there was a drug store in the market.

Drug stores, like most other stores in Cameroon, had thin inventories and half empty shelves, but they usually stocked what was necessary. There were four pharmacists behind a long counter and we were the only customers. The ibuprofen we bought was made in Nigeria, big fat pink pills that didn't look like anything I had bought before, but two of them gave me immediate relief.

It was 3:00 PM when we got back from the market and we all felt overheated and exhausted. We turned on the air conditioners in our rooms and napped until dinner. We were expecting to hear from a colonel in Maroua, whom Nia had told us was going to arrange our trip to the north, but he never showed up.

Just after breakfast next morning, two men drove into the courtyard in a Toyota Land Cruiser. The driver fit my image of what a colonel should look like, and I thought perhaps, this was the colonel that we had been waiting for. He was a tall light skinned Moslem with a very military bearing, but there was no insignia of rank on his uniform. He stood back however, with a pleasantly neutral expression on his face while the other man did the talking.

The other man was smaller and darker and very verbal and effusive. He reminded me of an insurance salesman as he placed his briefcase on the table. He was actually the boss, a travel agent, and my "colonel" was his driver. We never learned what happened to the colonel we were expecting to meet, but I guess if there really had been a colonel, he simply passed us off to this travel agent, whose name was Dabala Dieudonne. They had driven from Maroua to meet us and talk about our plans for the next week.

Dabala laid out an itinerary that included an overnight stay in Waza National Park, a visit to Chad, and several hill villages in the Mandora mountains along the Nigerian border. He included food and accomodations, transportation with a driver, and a guide who would accompany us as well. The price for the entire package was seven hundred and fifty thousand CFAs (fifteen hundred dollars). That was obviously an impossible amount since it would require all of our money and we would have no way of getting back to Buea. Traveling with Nia was a mostly pleasant experience, but it was expensive because in addition to his salary, every other expense we had was doubled.

We negotiated a price of four hundred and eighty thousand CFAs for our week in the north. We rose considerably in Dabala's estimation when we chose to eat African food in preference to European food. He hugged us with affection. We could leave immediately and ride with him to Maroua in the Land Cruiser.

We left immediately, and drove north for nearly four hours on the straight, narrow, badly paved road that was the main route to the north. We seldom saw any other vehicles. It was an area of limited rainfall called the Sahel, a transition zone one to two hundred miles wide between the Sahara desert and the grasslands to the south. It extended on our right across Chad and Sudan to the Red sea. To our left were the mountains of the Nigerian border, where the Sahel turned north, skirting them before resuming its westward course to the Atlantic Ocean. Our driver stopped at a Mosque to say his prayers, and several times to allow me to photograph small settlements or striking landscapes: thorn trees with their dramatic jagged branches, and once an overloaded truck which had tipped on its side.

CH 7

Maroua, Lake Maga, & Chad

We passed an army checkpoint just before Maroua. We must have looked respectable because we were waved through without having to show our papers. The avenue into Maroua was wide and flat and tree lined in the French fashion; long rows of handsome, evenly spaced, neen trees with feathery leaves that resembled our locust trees. Goats wandered everywhere. There was little four-wheeled traffic, but the road was filled with scores of light motorcycles carrying passengers.

One could see a great distance along the avenue. It had wide dirt sidewalks without curbs and businesses were set well back from the road surface. We turned into the courtyard of a hotel named the "Feti". Dabala conducted us into a large covered patio behind a courtyard where several tables of men were watching an Africa Cup Football match on television. The patio also served as the Feti's restaurant. We took a table and filled out our registration forms with our passport information for the room clerk, who was also the waiter, laundry person, and general factotum. There was a large cage at the front of the patio with a parrot that continually wished us "Bonjour".

The rooms were arranged in lines behind the restaurant and were fortunately air conditioned since the temperature was in the nineties the whole time we were in Maroua. When we had settled into our rooms, we went back to the dining area and discussed our plans for the next week with Dabala over beer. The Feti Hotel would be our base. There would be day trips from there and one longer four day trip, during which we would check out of the Feti and travel around the north, finally returning to the Feti once more at the end of our excursion.

Food at the Feti was limited to fish and rice or chicken and rice except at breakfast which was always a plain omelette and bread. The beer however was cold and good as always. Nia usually watched television in his room while Lorna and I drank beer in the dining room after dinner. On our first evening there, a young woman took a table near us to watch the television. She was dressed in a gray business suit and I thought she was a young professional of some kind.

I addressed her in French and asked her if she was on vacation. No, she lived nearby and spoke English. She told us her name was Maggie and we became friends. While we were in Maroua, Maggie came every night and sat with us. She knew as much about American politics as many Americans. She needed a job and hoped that Dabala might hire her, but all of Dabala's employees were members of his own family.

One night as I bemoaned our limited menu, Maggie offered to guide us to a place where we could buy grilled lamb. She walked between Lorna and me with our arms firmly linked. She led us for a half-mile through a dark residential section of walled streets. We passed her home on the way and she took us through a gate into a courtyard where she lived with her sister, who was a schoolteacher, and her little nephew. They basically lived in the courtyard eating and cooking there, but they slept in little rooms off the courtyard with pieces of cloth hung in place of doors. After meeting Maggie's family we continued through further dark streets until we finally emerged onto another avenue that parallelled the boulevard on which our hotel was located. It was a busy thoroughfare with loud music emanating from several nightclubs, and large groups of strollers moving along the broad sidewalks.

There were no streetlights, but the street was lit both by light from the clubs on the other side, as well as the vendors' cooking flames on our side. We stopped at a vendor that Maggie knew and after introductions we sat on sidewalk benches while he grilled orders of the surprisingly tender morsels of lamb for very little money. When we had eaten our fill, we walked back the way we had come, this time holding hands in a more leisurely stroll. Nia, who had been watching a soccer match at a nearby bar, returned to the Feti and joined us for beer on the restaurant terrace.

Early the next morning, Dabala came by just as we were finishing breakfast. He was ready to guide us to the tannery, the blacksmith's, and the great market at the center of the town. We set off at a fast walk. The leather workers occupied a large field on the other side of our avenue about half a mile toward the city center. There were holes in the ground full of vile smelling chemicals and stacks of skins and drying racks. The workers wore Arabic dress and either squatted or sat on the ground as they fleshed the skins. We met their chief and were told that he was a hundred years old but he looked so much younger that I was skeptical.

As we were leaving the tannery one of the workers, a skinny man with wild hair and trousers that were too short, got up and stood in front of me, his hand outstretched and said, "Cadeau". He was asking for a present. I had a twenty-five CFA coin in my pocket, a brass copper coin the size of a nickel and worth about as much. I presented it to him and walked quickly on. Behind me I heard his coworkers laughing at him.

We continued along the wide flat avenue for nearly another mile to the center of the city located on the other side of a straight truss bridge.

It spanned a wide riverbed that was completely dry. The center of town consisted of several concrete municipal buildings, one of which housed an artisan's store that served as an entrance to a large native market that occupied several acres under the neen trees by the river. Behind the market a strange hill rose with an unusual shape. It consisted of a pyramid of dry soil a couple of hundred feet high and it was the only hill in an otherwise flat landscape.

We looked first through the artisan's store that consisted of small stands selling jewelry or native clothing. We met the first white people we had seen in in several days, a missionary couple from the Midwest. The wife prided herself on being an astute shopper and told us that she always offered half of any asking price. However, there is really no substitute for knowing what local people will pay for things they want to buy, and after we had learned the true prices of things, we realized that the missionary lady was still paying twice as much as things were worth. The merchants had anticipated her technique. On the other hand it is not always fair to extort the lowest price possible, if by doing so you are taking advantage of a person's poverty simply to satisfy one's vanity in being a "smart trader".

We moved through the market without making any purchases. As in Guider, people had come long distances to sell there, many from Nigeria, the Central African Republic, or Chad. Far in the back of the market at the base of the strange hill, the blacksmiths sat on the ground, working at their craft. They had made some very beautiful daggers, and I bought one for five hundred CFAs (about one dollar). We bought strong fiber-impregnated bags to carry our purchases that included several plastic liters of water, samples of native produce that Lorna wanted to draw, and some interesting fetishes from the dealers in witchcraft. At noon, we flagged down five motorcycle taxis to take us back to the Feti. The roadway near the center of town was thronged with motorcycles, all moving from thirty-forty MPH without benefit of stoplights or policing.

The broad sidewalks carried a steady stream of people to and from the center. We had just crossed the bridge from the market when I saw a completely naked man walking towards us through a crowd of other pedestrians, and it surprised me that not a single person seemed to notice him or react in anyway to his presence in their midst. That evening when we told Maggie about him she told us that he was a

47

familiar sight to people who live in Maroua and shrugged as she asked us, "What can one do with such people?"

Back at the Feti we wanted to go to our rooms, but Lorna couldn't find our key, which she had been carrying. There were no duplicates available and so our desk clerk in company with two other men set to work with an assembly of axes, hammers, and crowbars and attacked our door for the next two hours. When they finally opened it they proceeded to replace the lock with a new one, all of which cost us six hundred CFAs (just over a dollar). They had just finished when someone returned the lost key that they had found in the market. It was a tardy miracle.

The money that Elsa gave us was disappearing fast and although our next week of traveling was paid for we would need more money to get back to Buea. I had kept some hundred-dollar bills as a secret reserve and I asked Dabala and Deli about changing them. Deli was Dabala's nephew, a handsome and hip young man who wore elegant designer sportswear. I didn't want Nia to know about the deal because I hoped he would show a little more financial restraint if he didn't know how much money I had.

A friend of Deli's met me and we worked out how many CFAs I would receive for five-hundred dollars. The exchange rate was very good considering that the dollar had been in free fall since our arrival in Cameroon and it was still dropping. News of the most recent rates had not found its way to the far north and I received almost twenty-five dollars more than the current exchange rate.

Despite my pleas for secrecy, Nia found out about the transaction and came walking in as the money was being exchanged. Of course he felt it was his duty to prevent me from being fleeced and he took over the transaction. He kept the extra twenty-five dollars and gave me the rest of the money that was in large bills. Although he used the money for everyone's benefit, I couldn't escape feeling somewhat resentful and didn't talk much for the rest of the day.

The next morning, Dabala appeared again during breakfast. It was a rotten breakfast. I had asked for a tomato and onion omelette and received an almost cold plain omelette. When I salted it the cracked plastic top of the saltcellar fell off and a couple of teaspoons of salt poured onto my eggs, while the parrot in his cage behind kept crying "Bonjour". It was a lie!

Every morning during our stay at the Feti, beggars came by during breakfast and stood politely near the entrance until signaled to come forward for alms. A tall blind grandfather, led by his tiny granddaughter, was the first to appear every morning. Almsgiving is an important part of Moslem culture, and we always tried to keep some small coins on hand for the beggars.

After breakfast, we left in the land cruiser for a trip to Lake Maga and Chad. We also planned to stop in the villages of a people known as the Pousse. The Pousse wear calabashes on their heads that resemble the shiny helmet liners that our soldiers wear, but which are much more colorful. They are carved from large gourds, and decorated with traditional designs. The Pousse inhabit bizarre houses unlike anything one sees elsewhere in the North, strange earthen domes that look like the abodes of giant insects.

We drove through the center of town, crossing the bridge where we had seen the naked man the previous day. From there we turned east on a road that was paved for only a few miles before becoming dirt. We rode for about thirty miles through flat country. Farmers were burning whatever remained of the crops from the fields, and the haze was thick and burned our eyes. It cleared after a few miles and we arrived at Lake Maga about an hour and a half after we had started out.

The road paralleled a fifteen-foot high dike that was several miles long that turned what had been a wetland into a large lake. At a place where several men had gathered we stopped and climbed onto the dike. Two truckloads of soldiers armed with assault weapons passed on the road behind us. There were seven or eight pirogues, each about four feet wide and twenty feet long, drawn up at the water's edge, and before us as far as we could see the waters of Lake Maga stretched.

Dabala negotiated with the boatman and the four of us climbed into one of the long boats. Two men operated it; one ran the outboard motor while the other worked the tiller. We set off and from time to time each of the men took a turn bailing. Twenty minutes later, we had lost sight of land, but in another ten minutes we were able to see the coast of Chad before us.

We came to a fisherman's shack near the water's edge. The fishermen were dressed in rags and animal skins and allowed their pictures to be taken, after we had "dashed" their chief, i.e. paid him two thousand

CFAs (four dollars). Without a common language, there was little reason to spend much time there.

We took leave of the fishermen and headed for an island where hippopotami usually congregated. There were no navigational aids that we could see, so we assumed that our boatmen set our course by the sun, but at high noon every direction looked the same. Nevertheless, after about twenty minutes, we could see a great disturbance on the water on the horizon, and soon the island came into view. There must have been twenty or thirty of the great beasts churning up the water in such a way, that it reminded me of my first sight of whales blowing in the distance. We had heard that they could be very dangerous, so we only came close enough for photographs, before heading for the shore where our vehicle waited.

We were out of sight of land when our motor failed for the first time. The boatman brought it back to life but it failed again in less than a minute. This was repeated several times during the next fifteen minutes, but finally it stopped and couldn't be started again. There were several short lengths of wood, laying about the bottom of the boat, which we picked up and put into service as oars.

We rowed for nearly an hour before the shore came into view. After that we alternated periods of rowing with periods when we stood up and waved and shouted. Finally, someone on land saw us and sent another boat to the rescue. We transferred to the other boat and quickly returned to land leaving our hapless boatmen to their own devices.

We had expected to visit the market and nearby villages of the Pousse next, but when we returned to our vehicles, there were a group of army officers talking with Dabala and our driver. Riots had broken out at the market between the millet growing Pousse and the rice growing Magas, and the military had closed off the entire area.

The day was hot and we were thirsty and heated from our exertions. Dabala took us to a nearby inn where we could refresh ourselves. The inn matched my conception of what a desert outpost of the French Foreign Legion would look like: barren, with everything the color of sand. The dining room, however, was cool, with formica-top tables and tubular metal chairs.

Dervla Murphy, who trekked in Cameroon with her daughter Rachel and a packhorse named Egbert in the nineteen eighties, and wrote about her experience in her book titled_Cameroon with Egbert, commented on the Cameroonian soft drinks sold under the brand name "Top". She wrote that they were "loathsome, ersatz fruit juices dyed a sinister orange or green". This was our first experience with an establishment where the superior Cameroonian beer was not available. Other Muslim establishments in the north had always accommodated us by sending someone out to get beer, but here we were isolated.

I ordered the evil-looking Pamplemousse (grapefruit flavored) for myself. The men in our group followed suit. Lorna ordered a Coca Cola. Despite the bizarre color, I found the drink extremely refreshing. Dabala was upset that his plans for our day had to be aborted, and he tried to make up for it by taking us to a real African restaurant for lunch when we got back to Maroua. We agreed, but first I wanted to go back to the market where I had bought the dagger the day before, in order to buy more of them. They were beautifully made and represented an enormous amount of work. The knifemakers used discarded automobile rims, which they sawed into small pieces and melted down. As the melted metal cooled, they hammered and shaped it into the proper shape for knife blades. The blades were then sharpened and sometimes, inscriptions were added. Hilts had to be carved from wood and fitted to the tangs. Finally leather scabbards had to be cut and sewn to complete each piece. At a cost of only one or two dollars they made great gifts to bring back to our friends in the U.S.

Lorna also wanted to make some purchases at the market. She liked the scarves with checkered design that Moslems wear that had become so familiar to Americans, since our involvement in the Middle East. Our driver, the man we had thought was a Colonel, was a Moslem from Kousseri, a town north of Maroua. He knew exactly the place at the market where such scarves were sold. Lorna bought six for three dollars apiece, and we set off for the strange hill, where I could find the blacksmiths.

It looked like a pile of sand, seventy or eighty feet high, and it was easy to see, in an otherwise flat landscape. We found fifteen or twenty workers, sitting on the ground and busily engaged in their tasks. When I announced my intentions to buy "*beaucoup de couteaux*", I was mobbed with competing artisans, each one extolling his own products over the work of his rivals. Many of the knives had decorations or dates on the blades and those were the ones I chose. I bought about a dozen in all for one or two dollars each and made my escape from the mob of blacksmiths, many of whom followed me for some distance before losing hope of making a sale.

Dabala took us to a restaurant that was located on a long avenue that paralleled the avenue of our hotel. We entered it through a long narrow hall that opened onto a crowded, trellis-shaded courtyard. Most of the hotel restaurants we had eaten in had served a menu limited to chicken, fish or eggs with rice or french fried potatoes. Dabala had taken us to an African restaurant that served the comfort foods that Cameroonians are brought up on. There were plates of large, turnip like yams, platters of plantains that had been sliced and fried in palm oil, and Fufu, which is a dumpling made from corn flour that accompanies soup or sauce. One breaks the Fufu into pieces and uses it like bread to scoop up the liquid. Dabala and Nia ordered Achoo, a porridge that looks like cream of wheat. The waitress used the bottom of a ladle to make a hole in the Achoo and spooned into it a ladleful of yellowish oil that included bits of meat. The waitress told Lorna and me that she didn't think we would like it, so we ordered Fufu and pepper soup made with chicken—spicy but good!

It was an especially hot day, even for a region where hot days are the norm. When we got back to our hotel I wrote up some notes I had made and cooled off with beer for the rest of the day. Lorna repaired to our airconditioned room and worked on her sketchbook. In the evening, after dinner, we sat with Maggie and discussed the state of the world.

CH 8

Waza, Rhumsiki, and the Maribout

Vulture Feathers

Next morning, Dabala came during breakfast. He brought along a tall slender young man who I guessed to be in his late twenties, and whom he introduced as his nephew, Koji. Dabala was apparently a man of many affairs and he had other obligations, so Koji was taking over as guide for the remainder of the trip. He assured us, however, that Koji spoke very good English and that we would all meet again in a few days when we got back from our trip to the north. He hugged each of us with fervor before we climbed into our vehicle and went off with Koji.

The plan was to make a three-day circuit of the north, spending the first night in Waza National Park and then heading into the Mandara mountains to spend the next night in Mokolo, a city of nearly a hundred and fifty thousand people twenty kilometers from the Nigerian border.

We planned to spend the second and last night of our trip in the picturesque village of Rhumsiki, which over looked a deep valley that marks the boundary of Cameroon with Nigeria. We rode in a sturdy 4x4. Nia occupied the front seat, and chatted in French with our driver who now wore Muslim clothing, a light blue caftan with a matching pillbox hat. He no longer resembled a colonel. Lorna and I sat in the next row of seats with Koji our guide in the seat behind us.

Periodically, Koji launched into explanations of the culture and history of the various groups of peoples living in the regions through which we were traveling. He spoke in long segments that he had obviously memorized verbatim from guidebooks. If we asked him a question, he would often lose his place and have to begin again with an exact repetition of what we had just heard. Koji was tall and slender with a long neck, a youthful face, and a serious and earnest manner that Lorna and I found endearing. We thought he was younger than he actually was, and we were surprised when he later told us that he had a wife and four children in Rhumsiki.

As we left Maroua, we drove north along the same two-lane highway that we had followed ever since we came down from the hills surrounding N'Gaoundere. The farther north we traveled, the drier the land became. As we had passed from Adamoua province into the northern provinces surrounding Garoua and Maroua, trees had become fewer and different, like the thorn trees, which were better suited to the dry conditions. Termite mounds were more frequent, and many of them were as high as seven or eight feet. The region north of Maroua was called Province de L'Extreme Nord.

We were looking forward to our stay in Waza National Park and we could have been there by early afternoon, but we made a side excursion to a mountain village called Oudjila. It was still midmorning when we took a left turn onto a wide and level dirt road that led into the mountains. We had driven only a mile or two when we came upon an area planted with neen trees, large mature trees spaced at fifty-foot intervals, as beautiful as the maple trees of a New England village. We had seen similar trees in Maroua, and apparently many of the large towns in the north had undergone a beautification campaign, probably about forty years ago, during President Ahidjo's administration.

Ahidjo was a northerner from Garoua who ruled Cameroon from its independence in 1960 until he turned the country over to Paul

Boya, the present ruler, in1980 while he visited France for medical treatment. After Boya consolidated his hold on the country, Ahidjo was sentenced to death in absentia to prevent his return.

We were entering a large town called Mora. Although it had a population of a hundred and sixty thousand people, they were diffusely spread throughout a wide area, and we saw few public buildings with the exception of schools. We passed a school where students were gathered in a mass formation of files and columns. They looked very impressive in their uniforms, blue shirts and trousers for the boys, and blue dresses with wide white collars for the girls. As they marched into the buildings, they swung their arms in exaggerated arcs.

We stopped at a small market to buy fruit and bottled water before resuming our trip. After Mora the road gradually became very rough and began rising steeply. The higher we went the worse the road got until it seemed that our vehicle was clawing its way up impossibly steep grades. On some turns the road fell away for a thousand feet or more and we held our breath for fear that our breathing might destabilize the vehicle and send us crashing into space.

Oudjila occupied the summit of the mountain. It was a village of a few hundred people, all of which were related to one another, forming an extended family or clan. There were about two dozen small, round, buildings with the characteristic conical grass roofs of the region, and a larger building with many extensions of rooms and passages in which the ruler lived with his sixty wives and their offspring. A tall young man with white shirt and dark trousers greeted us. He told us that he was the eighth son of the family and that he attended law school in Mora.

He collected a two thousand CFA note from each of us and conducted a tour of what he called the palace. The brick walls that formed the rooms and passages were smeared with mud that had dried to form a hard smooth surface. The rooms were devoid of furnishings except for some large earthenware pots used for cooking. During our tour we passed several small groups of wives who held out their hands to us for cadeaux (presents). All of the women we met wore simple blouses with their brightly patterned wraparounds, although post cards and tourist pictures of this area usually depict the women as bare-breasted.

Before we left the village, we met the chief, who sat apart with his important advisors on a circle of rocks overlooking the valley below.

He was a man in his fifties or early sixties who dressed in the style of an Afghan warlord. He exhibited an aura of immense dignity, as he smoked his pipe and chatted with his advisors. He greeted us in a perfunctory manner, and then ignored us and resumed his discussions while we photographed him.

It took more than an hour to return to the main road, and it wasn't until late afternoon that we reached Waza. There we were accomodated in individual shelters built in the local architectural style, replete with conical grass roofs. They were larger than usual, however, and they were made with cemented fieldstone instead of sundried bricks. Lorna and I shared a double bed that was enclosed by mosquito net that draped from the center of the roof fifteen feet above us. We unpacked and rested awhile, but dinner was still two hours away, and there was time and sufficient daylight remaining for us to begin our explorations of the park.

We drove to the administration building and met our guide. He was a very black man of approximately my size and weight, 5'8" and a hundred and fifty pounds. He wore a khaki colored uniform without insignias and his cheeks were marked with ritual scars. He spoke only French, in which I asked him many questions about the reserve. There was a lot of burning taking place throughout the reserve and we wonderered about the reason for it. His answer was succinct: "*pour qu'on vois les animaux!*" *(so you can see the animals!).*

The reserve with its scattered trees was the beginning of a plain that continued for thousands of miles across Chad and Sudan to the Red Sea. I photographed vultures perched on trees, patiently waiting for their next meals, and large flocks of guinea hens or *pintades* as they are called in French. We saw several antelopes, but we didn't have time to look for any other animals.

I had been taking pictures of the African sunset across the plain until it got too dark for any more photographs. Night falls quickly so close to the equator. It was almost dark when we disturbed a large male lion lying in the grass just ten feet from the road. He stood and looked at us for an instant and then turned away and disappeared in three large bounds.

That evening we went for dinner to an African restaurant in the town of Waza. There was no moon and the roads were very dark. The restaurant was dimly lit on the outside and even more dimly lit in the large room we entered. We sat in large upholstered chairs arrayed on the perimeter of the room and gave our orders to the waitress cum cook, cum owner. I ordered Guinness beer which was a change from the lighter "33" or the Castel that I usually drank. The Cameroonian Guinness was stronger and richer flavored than the Guinness I was used to. For our dinners we ordered Capitaine, the ubiquitous Nile perch of Cameroon, along with rice and plantains. The restaurant seemed full, although we could barely see our fellow customers in the dim light.

The night was cool and we slept well. Next morning we were up early in order to visit the waterholes again. This time, there were many antelope, ostriches, cranes and more vultures. We walked in places where elephants had left their enormous footprints in the hardened mud, but the elephants themselves were absent, having left to find water forty kilometers to the east. At one waterhole our driver and our guide made their ablutions, faced Mecca and then knelt to their prayers which took them about ten minutes.

We came to an area where there were giraffes. We could see them in the distance where they looked like they were the size of ants. We stopped our vehicle and our guide asked me to accompany him. We walked about two miles across fields scored with deep dried furrows from the passage of elephants and through light brush to get as close to the giraffes as possible. There was a large group feeding from the tops of the acacia trees and I counted twenty-seven, some of which were congregated in what seemed to be family groups.

We moved on from the reserve around midmorning because, considering the condition of the road, we faced a long drive of nearly a hundred and thirty kilometers to reach Mokolo, our next stop. The roads were very rough, limiting our top speed to twenty-five kilometers per hour. It was mostly mountain driving but nothing was as scary as the road to Oudjila had been. Mokolo was a fairly large city with a population of a hundred and forty thousand. It was the most suburban-feeling place that we had been in since we left the United States. We stayed at an airconditioned inn, next to a large filling station on a main street. The Africa Cup games were being played in Tunisia at the time and the Cameroon Lions in their yellow, green, and red colors, the colors of the Cameroon flag, were playing South Africa that night. The large dining room was filled with pumped up fans. Nia wore a jersey in the team colors and the beer began to flow. Everybody was buying rounds of "33s" which had printed special labels with pictures of the players. I lost track of the number of bottles I drank, but Cameroon won and the next day I was hung over and hoarse from screaming.

As we gassed up the next morning, we watched a street full of men and women dressed in neat business attire, walking quickly in the same direction, presumably toward the place where their offices were located. Leaving the town, we passed many detached bungalows that were probably occupied by civil servants, since they seemed to do better than most other people in Cameroon. A large water project and much road building was taking place in the region and I had watched the game the previous evening with a group of civil engineers from Buea who were involved with it.

We completed our circuit of the north with a visit to Rhumsiki. Although its distance from Mokola wasn't great in absolute terms, we didn't arrive there until nearly noontime. The road into Rhumsiki overlooked a deep valley that separated Cameroon from Nigeria, and looked more like a lunar landscape than anything I have ever seen on earth. Projecting from the floor of the valley were large rounded eminences, some as high as 800 feet. They were the remains of ancient lava columns that were left behind after the softer stone of the mountains had eroded. They looked unclimbable. Entering Rhumsiki, we saw at the side of the road a large gazebo on a promontory that seemed like an ideal place to take photographs. We stopped, and Lorna, Nia, and I climbed a flight of steps to reach it. I had only taken one picture when the battery in my camera died. My charger was back in Buea because I had been too thoughtlessly concerned with traveling as light as possible, with now, the result—a useless camera.

We found our inn and checked in, ate lunch and began our explorations of the town. Koji started off the afternoon by leading us to the house of the coppersmith. It was far off the road and we had a long walk to get to it. We crossed a wide field and then we followed a narrow path through the bush to a group of low buildings where the coppersmith lived. He had a large extended family, many of which were in evidence. That included several wives.

We paid his eldest son two thousand CFAs for each member of our group to see a demonstration of the art of coppersmithing. Several of the men of his family joined to watch. Squatting opposite me was the most wasted human being I had ever seen: a tall man who was little more than a skeleton clothed in a thin, tightly-stretched skin. It was painful to look at him and we wondered if perhaps he was a victim of kwashiorkor, the wasting disease.

We watched as the oldest son began the work of the coppersmith. He used wax to carve a mounted figure on a rearing horse, like the knight of a chess set. He covered it with clay that he packed around the model in order to make a mold. Then he led us a few hundred yards to an area where there were small fires burning in depressions in the ground. There, he filled a crucible with copper ore, added sufficient tin to make brass, and heated the metal over the fire until the resulting brass was liquid. It took nearly a half-hour to liquefy, during which he vigorously worked a hand bellows. Once the metal became liquid, he heated the mold, poured out the wax, and filled it with the molten metal. When it had cooled sufficiently he broke away the mold to reveal the figure he had cast. Unfortunately, the horse had only one leg, and it would have to be melted down and recast.

As we returned along the narrow path back to our vehicle, three of the wives passed us, looking very attractive in the brightly colored wrap-arounds that they wore over short-sleeved white blouses. They were each wearing large, elaborate, earrings of solid gold and they exuded youth and vitality. I was admiring their earrings and considering whether their complexions enhanced the gold, or if it was the other way around, when one of the women cast a side long glance at me from the corner of her eye and smiled. She knew that I thought she was beautiful.

The highlight of our day was our visit with the Marabout, known locally as the *Sourcier Au Crabe*. He was an old man in his eighties and well known throughout Cameroon; our friend Maggie in Maroua had known of and recommended him. His name was Tije Kidi and he was tall and light-skinned, perhaps six foot three. He had a long face and a full head of white hair and he wore what looked like an Irish knit sweater and blue trousers. He was remarkably vital for his age. As we walked to the large hut where he entertained visitors, we passed his wife, a short and wizened woman who was sitting under a tree, shelling a large pile of what they call groundnuts (peanuts).

We each had questions for the Marabout, who practiced an ancient Nigerian method of divination using a crab. After we paid an assistant one thousand CFAs for each question we wanted to pose, we were ushered into the sorcerer's presence. The sorcerer picked up his crab, which he fed on three grains of wheat per day, and placed it in a pot which he covered while he made certain incantations. He then paused for an interval after which he uncovered the pot. It was considered to be a very good sign if the crab had moved, especially if it had moved a lot, but if the crab remained immobile the consequences would be disastrous.

I went in first. I'm a skeptic, but I'll always go along for some fun. Lorna wanted me to find out if the book we planned to write would be successful. The Marabout's answer surprised me. "You will be successful," he announced in very good English, "but you must be sure to print enough copies to satisfy the great demand that you will find. "And someday," he continued, you will come back to Cameroon."

Nia and Lorna took their turns with the Marabout, while I sat with the Marabout's wife eating some of the groundnuts she was shelling. She told me that she was a Methodist and asked where we were from. Most Cameroonians guessed we were either French or Germans. "*Etats Unis*" I told her, and she nodded. She laughed often. Somewhere in the distance there was drumming. She stood up and began to dance and she signaled for me to get up and dance with her. Nia and Lorna came out and were surprised to find us both stepping energetically to the rhythm.

Nia and his wife Justina wanted a child, but were having difficulty conceiving. Nia asked the Marabout's advice for solving this problem. The Marabout told him that the problem arose from bad feelings that festered in his wife's family, and that he needed to go to her father with gifts of wine and food, which would resolve the matter. Nia worried that it would cost a lot of money because his father-in-law was fond of a particular French wine that was very expensive.

When Lorna spoke with the Marabout, she asked about the success of our book. He had already answered this question for me and he laughed. Why, he wanted to know, had we waited so long to do this thing? If I had begun writing at a younger age, we could already have been enjoying the fruits of success.

When we left the Marabout and his wife, there were still more than two hours of sunlight remaining, and we set off to visit some of the other craftsman of the village. We acquired an entourage of children who wanted presents. Unfortunately, we had spent all of our money and there was nothing to give them. One by one, as they realized that there was nothing to gain, they dropped off, until there remained only a single rather pleasant young man who informed us that his name was Michael Jordan.

He spoke French but his English was excellent also. He was very likable and he walked along with us, keeping up a lively conversation, while we looked at traditional pots at the pottery and weaving at the Tisserand's. One of the weavers was very drunk and he wanted to sell us the portable spinning device that he used to turn cotton into thread. He followed us everywhere, and I found him particularly obnoxious because he stood too close to me and was constantly whining, but Michael was finally able to persuade him to leave us alone.

We left Rhumsiki early the next day and returned to Maroua. For one final evening we sat with Maggie and drank beer while we talked about our circuit of the extreme north province. The Cameroon Lions were playing against Nigeria. Nia went to another local bar to watch the game. It ended in a tie. Early next morning we loaded our packs and walked to the bus company for our trip back to N'Gaoundere.

We took a small minibus with twenty or so other passengers. As we were getting off the bus in Garoua we met a young man from the US wearing a Colgate sweatshirt who had been our fellow passenger since Maroua. His name was Brian and he was a Peace Corps worker whose job was in forestry in the far north. He was taking a few days of vacation and was on his way to visit other Peace Corps members stationed in Kribi on the south coast. He was looking forward to watching a tape of the recent Superbowl game that one of them had just received in the mail. He gave me the news that New England had won.

Garoua's temperature was in the high nineties, a perennial subject for conversation. Brian told us that his parents were coming to visit him in two months, a time when temperatures in the north often reached a hundred and twenty degrees or more. Someone mentioned the Peace Corps worker's parent who had recently been killed by an elephant, and someone else pointed out the far greater danger that share cabs presented.

CH 9

Return to Buea

When we got back to N'Gaoundere, we checked back into the Hotel du Rail. While we were settling in, Nia went off on a shopping trip. He was gone for a long time. Dinnertime arrived and he still hadn't returned, so Lorna and I engaged two motorcycletaxis and went off to find dinner. The center of town was three or four miles away. Most of the restaurants were concentrated in a single block, defined by two parallel main streets.

There was an African restaurant that our guidebook had recommended that was famous for its ndole, a sauce made from bitter leaves and groundnuts, which can be used with either meat or fish. The restaurant was so crowded that we couldn't find a seat, so we left and walked down the block. Our guide recommended another restaurant called "La Plaza", but indicated that it was very expensive and I had doubts that it could fit our budget.

We found "La Plaza" on the next street, and surveyed the interior through the glass door at the entrance. It looked elegant. There was a large room with about thirty tables, snowy white tablecloths, handsome place settings, candles, and meticulously folded napkins. Perhaps we were early, but there was not a single customer in evidence. We started to leave, but just then a voice out of the dark spoke to us in French. Two men were drinking at a table on the terrace, and the one who spoke was a Lebanese who owned the restaurant. "Est-ce que vous aimez entrer?", he had asked. "Trop cher" we responded ((too expensive).

He proceeded then in English, and told us that his prices were very reasonable. He was sure, he added, that we would be surprised. We were indeed surprised when we found the best steak and French fries that we had had in Cameroon, with glasses of very good French wine, and excellent service from a solicitous waitress. Our bill was no higher than we usually paid for indifferent meals at most of the hotels we stayed at. Perhaps he decided we were not rich, and made a special price for us. We stopped by his table on the way out, and he told us about two art stores that he owned in Foumban. Foumban was the chief city in the Bamoun region of Cameroon, ruled by a sultan, and was famous for its great palace and as an important art center.

Our motorcycles back to the inn cost two hundred CFAs instead of the one hundred CFAs that we had paid earlier, because prices were higher after dark. We enjoyed speeding along the African roads in the moonlight; it felt adventurous and magical. Nia had waited for us to have his dinner, and we felt guilty about our elegant meal. We told him without elaboration that we had gotten something to eat in town. The Hotel du Rail was owned by Muslims and consequently did not have beer, but they sent a motorcycle courier to fetch some for us with which we passed the evening. The train for Douala did not leave until six o'clock the following evening.

At breakfast we encountered two French women at the next table whom we had met the previous afternoon when they arrived by car from the airport. One was an ethnologist, who was accompanied by her sister, and who had written several books during a twenty-year study of the peoples of the area. They talked about their work, but since neither of the women spoke English, the discussion was carried on in

French. They had been flown in to attend a meeting at the University of N'Gaoundere in honor of a very old friend.

We needed supplies for the long railroad journey home, which was how we now thought of Buea. We hired three motorcycles to take us to town for a late brunch and the shopping we needed. In Cameroon, good bread, butter, cheese and other imported delicacies are scarce and usually sold only at boulangeries although, sometimes, one can find them at small stores designated as supermarches. Our map indicated that there is a supermarche a short walk outside the town and after brunch we set out to find it. Unfortunately, it was really a large native market that was misnamed on the map. After further searching, however, we found a small boulangerie where we could buy bottled water, bread, and cheese to sustain us on the long train ride back to Buea.

We still had a few hours to kill before train time, so we relaxed on the porch with fellow guests until it was time to go. When we left, Nia was unable to leave with us, since he had bought fifty pounds of onions for an upcoming party at Elsa's, and no driver would carry the extra load. We had no problem hiring two motorcycles, as we had only our backpacks to deal with. Nia did not show up at the station for another half-hour, which was how long it took him to find a driver who would try to steer with a huge bag of onions propped on his handlebars.

Lorna and I took our seats on the train but the conductor would not allow Nia's onions on the train as hand luggage. He insisted that the onions had to be shipped as cargo. That would cost extra. After a discussion of ten minutes that sometimes grew quite heated, Nia handed the conductor a few coins and told him, "Here is your beer". With that the conductor picked up the bag of onions, carried it to our seats, and helped Nia store it in the overhead rack. The sun was setting as the train began moving. We looked around us; family groups were sitting in facing seats, as we were. A few children played in the aisle as we settled in for our long trip. Three hours passed, and just when we were beginning to think that we might reach Douala by early morning the train stopped at a tiny station. Minutes dragged as we waited to resume our journey. The train gave a lurch and we thought we were on the move again, but it was only the beginning of a series of spasmodic jerks spaced further and further apart, like the death agonies of some great beast, until it finally expired in a hiss of escaping steam.

The night was very dark and except for a few indistinct figures moving on the platform, there was little we could see. Nia walked up to the front of the train to talk to the engineers. When he came back he informed us that a replacement locomotive was being sent from N'Gaoundere. The children on the train had by now fallen asleep in their parents' arms, and the rest of us settled down to wait in stoic resignation. It was well after midnight before the replacement engine arrived and we got moving again. It had taken us seven hours to complete what should have been the first three hours of our trip.

Just before we left Boston, Lorna had smoked what we hoped would be her last cigarette ever and she had since been relying on nicotine replacement tablets to mitigate the stress of tobacco withdrawal. Her stress level was rising, and she thought that perhaps hard candy would help. She gave some money to a woman who was a circulating vendor on the train, and who promised to bring her a large bag of it. Four hours passed as we slowly gave up hope of ever seeing that woman again, but it wasn't until five hours had passed that she finally showed up again with a large bag of toffee made in Nigeria. I joked that Nigeria was a very long distance to travel to, and return from, in only five hours. It certainly shows the lengths people in Cameroon will go to, if they can make a little money by providing some service.

The night seemed endless, but morning finally arrived and we found ourselves passing through a region of dense growth. Periodically, we caught sight of the Sanaga River, which closely paralleled the railroad, and looked deep and blue, a welcome change from the dry riverbeds of the north. Occasionally we saw a person, walking in a narrow path that cut through the undergrowth—a load on her head if it was a woman, or unencumbered if it was a man. At each stop, strolling vendors crowded the edge of the platform and did a brisk business from large trays that they carried on their heads. They sold oranges they had peeled, pineapples they had peeled and cored, or groundnuts (peanuts), which they had shelled and candied in clumps like peanut brittle.

Near Belabo, a town that marked the halfway point of our trip, the railroad changed from its southerly path that paralleled the Central African Republic, and turned west toward Yaounde and the coast. At one stop, a series of health hustlers got on the train. They had each memorized their particular sales pitch. When I was a child I lived across the street from the Bunker Hill Monument, and these hustlers reminded me of the urchins who memorized the history and facts about the monument, and spouted them in rapid monotone to tourists for a small coin.

The first entrepreneur to get on our train sold tiny packages of baking soda, which he extolled as a universal remedy for every health problem imaginable. Another entrepreneur sold pamphlets containing botanical information about healing herbs. He represented this as a business opportunity for a buyer who could find them locally and start his own business. Surprisingly, they each made sales in our car, before they got off at the next stop to take the train back and sell in the opposite direction.

We arrived in Yaounde at noon, tired, hungry and feeling deprived after so many hours on the train. We engaged a taxi to take us to the bus station, where we boarded a large modern bus for the four-hour trip to Douala. There, we caught a taxi to take us back to Buea. We made a stop at Zepol's, the unique and wonderful boulangerie that we had visited on our first day in Cameroon. After the narrow range of choice we had found for most of our meals in the North, the display of prepared delicacies for sale was so enticing that it felt like a dream. We chose from case after case of prepared sandwiches, pizzas, breads and croissants, including my favorite chocolate ones. We assuaged our deprivation with a two-day supply of food, and got back to our inn in Buea before dark.

Nia was homesick and sorely missed his wife, Justina. He departed for his home in Limbe as soon as we had removed our packs from the taxi. Lorna was suffering from nicotine withdrawal, and we had spent all the money we took North with us, down to the last few coins. When we telephoned Elsa, she came at once with Lorna's Commit pills and a hundred thousand CFAs (about $200.00) for our immediate needs. She could see how tired we were, and she left after a round of beer, promising to return in the morning.

CH 10

Daily life in Buea

Fung's family had welcomed us with kindness and tried to provide us with the experience of their country they thought we expected. They felt a sense of responsibility for our safety and wanted to watch over us as much as possible. Elsa feared that we might find Cameroon too challenging. She had met us in the U.S. when she visited for Clara and Fung's wedding, and was not reassured that we would be able to deal with the rigors of life in her country. She further assumed that we didn't know French, and felt sure that we would be cheated in the marketplace. She arranged for her brother Nia to be our keeper, and guide us in our visit to the North. I should have been grateful.

Instead, I was feeling angry and depressed. "There is not going to be a book!" I told Lorna. "It was supposed to be an adventure story, and not about some feckless idiot being dragged around Africa by his keeper". I felt like one of those phony mountain climbers, that have themselves hauled up mountains like sacks of potatoes, and I was feeling resentful all over again for every time Nia's bossy ways had made me feel like a child. I half realized that I was exaggerating and feeling sorry for myself, but I was very tired, and concerned about our finances. We had been in Cameroon for just over two weeks of what we had hoped would be a three to four month stay, and we had already spent half the money we had budgeted for the entire trip.

We had yet to embark on the most important part of our trip, which was our visit to Wum. Wum is the home of the Aghem people, where Fung's father had ruled. Elsa wanted her son Luke to accompany us, since Nia needed to return to his job in Limbe. Not only had Nia been another expense on our trip north, but we had also paid him sixty dollars a week for lost wages, and we could do no less for Luke. This was clearly financially impossible, and besides, we wanted to travel on our own.

When Elsa came by the next morning, we these things. We talked about our financial problems and our other expectations for the duration of our visit. I felt wonderfully restored by a good night's sleep and all my negativity had vanished. Elsa suggested that we could move into a guesthouse that the Protestant Church maintained and live there for less than half what we were paying at the OIC Hotel. Her only concern was that it wouldn't meet our standards. We convinced her that we would adapt to whatever conditions we found, and we moved that same day. I think that her visits to the United States gave her the impression that we had so much that we were too spoiled to be able to deal with less.

The long road up the lower flank of Mount Cameroon from the coast ended at a traffic circle a mile beyond our hotel. There, another road ran left and right, as if following a contour line around the mountain. Elsa and Paul lived with their sons in a small neighborhood of modern stone houses along the road to the left. The road to the right led to our guesthouse at the Protestant Center, which was next to a large school, and further, to the market area called Bueatown. The Protestant compound was spread along a hill above the road, in front of the main mass of the mountain, which behind it rose abruptly before disappearing into the haze above.

The guesthouse was a long stone building at the edge of the church compound, situated on a ridge above the school. It was a boarding school, and from our room we looked down on the boys' dormitories, separated from the girls' dormitories by a wide field. The assembled students, dressed in their blue shirts or skirts, marched there daily at sunrise to the beat of drums. However, these were not the first sounds of the day. Somewhere below the road was a prison, which we passed through often, when our shared taxis happened to take that route around town. It looked like an army camp, and many of the prisoners came out daily to work. Every morning we were waked up before sunrise by a contingent of guards who chanted cadences as they jogged by in formation. Mary Kingsley had written about this prison, having passed through it in 1895 in her climb of Mount Cameroon.

Our room was small but adequate with a desk by the window separating our two cots. There was a small bathroom with a shower. On some afternoons, we looked through the banana trees that grew wild on the hillside and watched the boys, washing their clothes in large tubs and cavorting naked in the showers, screened by their dormitories from eyes below, but unaware of those from above. The guesthouse had a shared kitchen with a gas stove, a sink, a refrigerator, and a few cooking tools and eating implements, which was presided over by Madame Magdalene Mbwaye. She was an imposing woman who insisted that anything out of place was returned exactly to its proper location, otherwise casting baleful glances at the offending party. There were usually about a dozen people in residence, not all of whom cooked, but those of us who did staked out territories in the refrigerator. Next to the kitchen was a dining room next to the kitchen where we ate and met our fellow roomers. At the OIC Inn, we had never met anyone who wasn't staff. At the guesthouse, however, we met and had long conversations with almost all of the other occupants.

On one side of the dining room, there were some rattan easy chairs with cushioned backs and seats. On the other side, a long table ran to a window, which was on the same side of the building as our room, overlooking the school. There were seats for sixteen at the table, but there were seldom more than two or three others present, except for occasional groups of mountain climbers and guides. The business manager, a slender and pleasant young man, was often around during the day, but at night one could find one or two of the guests working here, because the light in the rooms was too poor to read by.

We shopped for food in Bueatown, in a labyrinth of ramshackle sheds where we found chicken, rice, beans, vegetables and fruit for our dinner. We made a huge stew, large enough to last a couple of days. We extended it with additions whenever it was in danger of running out. The ordinary bread was a ubiquitous two-pound pullman loaf that was unsliced, and so rubbery that it was impossible to slice it until we discovered that we could make slices if we first froze it in the refrigerator. We bought beer from the nearest bar on the main road: six or eight .65 liter bottles, which seemed to grow heavier during our walk of nearly a mile back to the compound and up the steep gully which we took as a shortcut to the guesthouse.

When we brought our food to the common table on our first evening at the guesthouse, we found a scholarly looking man working at his laptop by the window. I guessed that he might be forty years of age. He had gray, curly hair and an intelligent, laid-back look that would not have been out of place at MIT. His name was Moses Nkwo, and he was the treasurer of Soweda, the Southwest Development Administration, which had its offices nearby. He was having a house built, and was living at the guesthouse while work was in progress.

He was one of the few people we met in Cameroon who smoked, because most could not afford the cost. He wanted to quit himself, and was very interested in Lorna's Commit pills that were helping her to give up cigarettes. We talked about Clara and Fung and our reasons for coming to Cameroon, and he was so interested that he contacted them directly by email and exchanged several messages with them. One evening when they telephoned us by cell phone, he was able to talk with them in person.

There was a morning when we met a young woman at breakfast who had travelled from Bamenda. She had arrived the previous afternoon in the pickup truck that made trips between church centers. She had found the trip so fatiguing that she had rested in her room until breakfast. She was slight and delicate, with a tiny waist and a full skirt. I thought that she looked too fragile to be traveling around Africa alone, but realized I was wrong when she gave me her card, which identified her as a Program Officer in a London-based NGO. She was engaged in an inspection tour and had been visiting an experimental spice garden in Bamenda. Her name was Isabelle Carboni, and she had grown up in West Africa. We asked her about Bamenda because it was our next destination, and we planned to stay at the church center where she had just stayed. She described the room she had rented there, very large and devoid of any furniture other than a bed.

While we were at the guesthouse, we met another European who had grown up in Africa. His name was Hans Sachs, and he had lived in Tanzania, where he had attended an English boarding school. He had also lived in Nairobi, where his father had lectured at the university. Hans was forty-six years old and married, with two sons. His entire life had been spent in Africa, except for the years that he had studied forestry in Gottingham.

He lived in Kumba, a town about thirty miles away, and was visiting Buea to meet an official whom he hoped could extend his contract in forestry management. Hans was slightly taller and proportionately heavier than I am, with a full, dark brown beard, flashing eyes, and a Germanic accent. He spoke with great intensity, and at times his words poured forth in a torrent. We talked for four hours after dinner, and continued the conversation for another two hours after breakfast the next morning as if we had never stopped.

Hans was living in Rwanda when the massacre took place, and he told us that he had never felt any sense of personal danger. He condemned the U.N. forces for what he called their feckless withdrawal from the beautiful country that he had loved, and he mourned many lost friends. We went on to talk about masks and the roles they played in the secret societies of the grasslands. He confessed that anytime he had ever worn a mask, he had felt something dark, lurking within himself; something that he sensed could take over his mind if he wasn't careful.

We shopped daily, and often we saw the same taxi driver around town that we had hired on our first day in Cameroon. His name was John, and he always waved to us. His taxi was in better shape than most, and we hired him when we could. We frequently shopped at Bendo's Boulangerie, two or three miles from our guesthouse, and approximately a mile past the OIC, where we had stayed previously. They sold bread that was a welcome change from the rubbery white loaves sold at the local markets. We did the rest of our shopping at the native market just down the road. The battery in my watch failed the day after our move, but I was able to find a replacement at a store in Bueatown.

A shortage of change for small purchases was a constant problem. No one had change, and our small money was used up so quickly that we were constantly trying to find more or retain what we had. It was surprising that we couldn't even get change from the Post Office. If we presented a 5,000 or 10,000 CFA note (equivalent to ten or twenty dollars) at an open market, the dealer would often take our money and disappear for fifteen or twenty minutes before reappearing with our change.

Elsa had been planning a large lawn party to thank the friends, neighbors, and family members whose contributions had enabled her to go to the United States at the time of Clara and Fung's wedding. Her principal focus at that time had been knee surgery. She was a highranking teacher in the school system, and although she was well paid by Cameroonian standards, she would have found it difficult to afford the operation that she needed without the assistance of her church.

We had planned to leave for Bamenda soon after Elsa's party, which was due to take place following church services on the upcoming Sunday. One afternoon during our last week in Buea, we heard an immense truck grinding up the road to our guesthouse. It was like nothing we had ever seen and it parked at the end of the house. It was like a huge earth-moving truck that had been modified to carry about twenty people. There were places for people to ride built into the chassis at various points. The monstrous vehicle rode on tires that were five feet in diameter. Its passengers were climbing out as we approached.

It was an entirely self-sufficient vehicle, equipped with extra tires, gas tanks, and other extra parts. We watched two passengers pull out a large awning mounted on a spring roller, while others assembled a field kitchen that had been stored in special built-in compartments, and within moments a meal was underway.

Most of the passengers were either retired couples or young people of college age. They were Australians or New Zealanders, and they had left London four months earlier to drive overland to Capetown. They had passed unmolested through some dangerous country, especially parts of Nigeria. However, most malefactors would be wary of tangling with such a large group.

They set up tents for the night, and used the guesthouse only for showers and laundry. Their website was travelafrica.com, which I accessed after we had returned to the United States. I was surprised to learn that their entire eight-month trip had cost them only six thousand dollars.

When Sunday arrived, we heard Nia's familiar voice, as he came looking for us to take us to church. He brought each of us a set of African clothing to wear, which he had secretly ordered for us while we were traveling in the North. Since Lorna always wore shirts with pants while traveling, she was not given the traditional female attire; instead she was dressed like me. Lorna is a beautiful woman who would look good in anything, but I would have preferred more feminine attire.

At the church there were several choirs, each occupying its own section of pews. Every choir member wore the unique skirt and headwrap that was the uniform of her own group. Most men wore business suits, although there were a few who dressed African. Some men and women were wearing what I called 'Protestant cloth', which was a bright-green fabric with the coat of arms of the church printed all over.

There were no empty seats in the church for the service that began at nine o'clock and ended at twelve. The liturgy resembled the Roman Catholic liturgy that I had learned as a child, and progressed in a logical fashion that did not seem overly long. The choruses were outstanding. At one point, Lorna and I were asked to stand, and we were introduced to the congregation.

When the church service ended, Nia drove us to Paul and Elsa's home for the party. We had heard much about Justina, his wife, but we met her for the first time only that morning when she rode with us to church. She was an attractive young woman in her late twenties, and now as we rode with her to the party, we all talked as if we had known one another forever.

Justina had just acquired a paying job in nursing, and Nia, who had paid for her schooling, was very pleased. He had often complained while we were traveling around the North that she worked for no money at a charity hospital. She enjoyed it, and he was afraid that she would stay there forever. It is unfortunate that jobs like nursing pay so little in Cameroon.

Paul and Elsa's house was screened from the street by a tall, dense hedge. There is a large yard between the fence and the house that was dominated by a strange palm tree that Paul planned to have removed because its crenellated trunk could easily harbor snakes. There were rows of seats for more than a hundred people under two long, free standing awnings that were set up in an ell shape. Tables loaded with food and drink filled the large central area.

Several chickens and a goat had been killed, and there were dishes loaded with roast meat, boiled yams, fufu, jamajama, and fried plantain. There were several cases of every major brand of beer: Castel, "33", Amstel, and Guiness, as well as French wine and hard liquor for those who preferred it.

People filled paper plates and returned to their seats, and socialized with their neighbors as they ate and drank. We recognized the woman who sold us tomatoes at the market, sitting with two friends in the row behind us. They were having a good time, laughing and talking about men. The youngest woman wanted to get married, but the older two were telling her stories to dissuade her. She wanted to know if we could find an American man for her, and we promised to try.

Paul and Elsa were occupied with their roles of host and hostess, so we circulated through the throng on our own and met many new relations, some of whom had traveled great distances to attend. An uncle from Wum was two hundred and fifty miles from home. He was a courteous man who lived for Jack Daniels, and became glassy-eyed as the afternoon progressed.

The weather was warmer than usual, but we were comfortable in African dress, and when the party broke up, we decided to walk back to our guesthouse. Paul had arranged a ride for us, but he understood when we told him we would enjoy the walk, which was less than two miles.

Ch 11

We flee to Bamenda

A few days later, we left for Bamenda. In a sense, it was a flight, because we wanted to escape the extreme protectiveness of our new relations, and find our way ourselves. Elsa rode with us to the motor park at mile 17, where assembled bus agencies ran connections to other parts of the country. Each line had its own ticket window in one of the low buildings surrounding the traffic circle. Nearby were the buses, modified window vans, with spaces for twelve to fourteen passengers. Most of them were white, with the names of their agencies emblazoned in large colorful block letters on all four sides. It was 9:00 A.M., but we were only the second people to buy tickets to Bamenda. We chose our seats and turned our packs over to men who were loading the bus, and watched while they lashed them to the roof.

Shortly thereafter, an older lady that Elsa was acquainted with took a seat in the row in front of us. She had been Fung's grade-school teacher when he was growing up in Buea, and she was on her way to Bamenda to visit her daughter, son-in-law, and three grandchildren. Lorna made her a present of a picture of Clara and Fung's wedding, and thtat was sufficient for her to take charge of us immediately. Only then did Elsa feel that it was safe to leave us.

Our bus filled very slowly, and long periods went by when no one appeared. The bus would not move until every seat had been sold. While we waited, we watched a steady stream of vendors, carrying their wares in enormous backpacks, or in large trays that they balanced on their heads. There were watches, rings, toys for children, pills for various conditions, toiletries and grooming supplies, cakes and candies, fruit, and grilled meat on sticks, which is called soya. There was an endless variety of goods for sale, and the passengers seemed to buy them readily, but not without spirited negotiation over prices.

As the morning wore on, we left our seats several times to walk around and stretch our legs. It was not until one o'clock that the last ticket was sold, and we began to feel hopeful when the driver pulled next to a pump at the gas station. It was only to engage in another interminable process, which was filling the gas tank by one drop at a time it seemed. This went on for more than half an hour, and involved repositioning the bus several times, in order to tip the gas tank to an angle that would accommodate a few more ounces.

It was one thirty when we finally got on the road, and we knew that we wouldn't arrive in Bamenda until long after dark. The luggage on the roof of the bus was piled so high that it could possibly tip over if we drove too fast. The road was a two-lane highway in reasonably good condition, but Bamenda was three hundred and eighty five kilometers (two hundred and thirty miles) away, and we had to make many stops. We came across several toll stations along the way, which consisted of a small booth and a few soldiers, using a spiked strip to block the road until the toll had been paid. At every stop there was a mob of vendors. At one of our first stops, a man was selling flashlights. He sold four to people on our bus, including one to Fung's former teacher, who was sitting in front of us. She bargained astutely, and the sale was only consumated when the bus was moving again, with the flashlight seller jogging alongside.

There were four rows of seats, and we sat in the third row. Four women with two babies sat behind us, and there was another baby next to the schoolteacher in front of us, but we never heard a sound from any of them, since mother's breast was always available. About three hours into the trip, we took a long rest stop at a small village that had a business strip on both sides of the road.

Lorna and Fung's teacher crossed the road to a restroom, where there was a small fee required, which Lorna paid for them both. I went into a bar and bought a wonderfully cold beer, which I consumed in about three draughts (remember, beer in Cameroon is sold in .65L bottles), and then bought a second one, and one for each of the ladies.

We had left Southwest Province and were passing through West Province, where only French is spoken, before re-entering the English-speaking part of Cameroon near Bamenda. When I had finished my beer, I left the ladies talking and walked back along the road towards where I had seen stands selling fresh fruit. I bought some very large avocados and a huge pineapple for the Cameroonian equivalent of about fifty cents.

The shadows of the hills around the road were lengthening as we got back on the road again. We rode another two hours to Bafoussam, the chief city of West Province. It was dusk. Bafoussam was a busy city with a business district that extended for more than three miles along a wide street, which rose and fell in gradual slopes. We pulled off the roadway and parked at the local office of the bus company. We were in Bamileke country. There is a unique style of architecture used there that is found nowhere else. Their roofs consisted of arrays of identical pyramids, constructed from sheet aluminum. The size of the roof determined the number of pyramids used. At one time they would have used pointed bundles of grass. This architecture was exemplified by the palace of the Fon of Bafoussam, which occupied a large area along the other side of the road from where we were parked.

Night had fallen by the time we left Bafoussam. It seemed particularly dark in the absence of streetlights. Several times the bus stopped to let people on and off, often, it seemed, when we were far from any evidence of human habitation. Someone would signal the driver to stop, and then climb out onto the road, and stride away into the night. How could they have possibly known where they were?

It was after 8:00 P.M. that we had our first sight of Bamenda. We came to a place where the wall of trees along the left side of the road fell away, and suddenly we saw the lights of the city, spread hundreds of feet below. "Isn't it beautiful?" Fung's teacher asked us. But before we could answer, the lights went out all over the city. Someone else said, "It happens all the time". We had arrived at Upper Station, a part of the city where all the bus agencies had their offices.

Our bus pulled into the parking area, and we climbed out into a moonless night. The darkness seemed total at first, but our eyes became accustomed to it and we found we could see quite well by the light of the stars. Almost directly overhead, the belt of Orion marked the equator, and the light from the billions of stars that make up the Milky Way left its soft streak in the night sky. The driver and a helper climbed onto the roof of the bus and began passing down luggage. Starlight was soon supplemented with flashlights and headlights from cars.

Fung's teacher's daughter and son-in-law had been waiting for three hours. We were introduced to them, and they kindly insisted on driving us to our destination, the Protestant Church Center. We first navigated down a series of switchbacks to the city proper, where we found a road that led through dark streets to the gated campus on the edge of the city. At first the campus seemed deserted, but we noticed a light in a building identified as the Administration Building. There we found a young woman who introduced herself as Patience, and told us that she had been expecting us.

Patience led us across the road to a line of low buildings with porches that ran their length, and doors that opened motel-style. She showed us into a very large room that contained a double bed, its sole piece of furniture. One could have held a dance in all the extra space. We thanked Fung's teacher and her daughter and son-in-law for all that they had done for us, and they left, shortly followed by Patience. We made a light supper from food we had brought, and went to bed immediately. The temperature dropped during the night, and in the morning we woke, huddled together for warmth.

In the morning we breakfasted on the fruit that we had brought on the road, and then went to find the business manager at the Administration Building. It was a square, two story building set on higher ground with its back to the road. It was an attractive modern building, and it used textures of stone and stucco in interesting ways. We found the entrance around the front, in a landscaped area of flowering trees and exotic shrubs. It had a large atrium, around which the building was designed. Conference rooms branched off the lobby, with framed testimonials from the many international organizations that had used the center. Several were from the State Department of the United States.

A wide, freestanding staircase led to a second-floor balcony, where other conference rooms and offices were located. Large African pots and carvings were displayed around the common areas. The manager's office was on the second floor. His door was open, and he was reading a newspaper. We stood by the door until he noticed us and waved us in. He was a broad man, with short grey hair and tortoise-shell glasses. He was wearing a blue and white striped shirt with an open collar, and his sleeves turned back over his forearms. We introduced ourselves and took seats.

He told us that a room would cost 8,000 CFAs a day ($16.00). We asked about meals, and he informed us that we could have breakfast for 1,000 CFAs each per day. We could also have dinner for 2,000 CFAs per day, whenever it was prepared, which was only when conferences were being hosted. We had initially planned to stay at the center for two weeks, and I offered to pay in advance. "Later, later", he said, as he waved me off expansively.

When we went back to our room, there was a tall, smiling young man waiting for us. "I am Che Aaron" he announced. "I'm here to help you move." We had been given an apartment at the front end of the house next door. It was large, attractive, and comfortably furnished. There was a kitchen that had a large kitchen sink with running water, and a gas range with an empty gas canister that Che promised to fill. We opened a cabinet and found all the necessary pots, pans, dishes, and eating utensils. The only thing missing was a refrigerator. We would have to make frequent shopping trips.

Che brought us sheets and towels and told us about himself. He did everything from plumbing to construction at the center, and he told us that his full name was Che Aaron Maryo. Lorna told him about Clara and Fung's wedding. It was both our credential and the reason we had come to Cameroon. It was Lorna's way of saying "I have a connection with you". We told him that Fung was very interested in African music, and Che told us proudly that he himself was a musician and songwriter. He had made a CD with his backup group that showcased his music, and he promised to bring us a copy. He took the gas canister to have it refilled, and we settled into our new quarters.

We made up our cots and put our clothes away. Lorna had a large wardrobe on her side of the room, while I had a large oversized dresser. There was a table that we could use for a desk, and several small occasional tables and chairs. Our bottled water was nearly gone, and we would need to make a shopping trip.

We found that there was a store called the Vatican Supermarket, located at the City Chemist's roundabout, about a half a mile from the Church Center. We left by the main gate, which was never closed, onto a street that ran left along the edge of the church property. Houses on our left were above the road, while those on our right occupied a deep gully. There were stands along the street selling bananas and avocados, and snacks of candied peanuts. We passed two small stores on the right where one could buy a few eggs, choose from a handful of groceries, or buy warm beer. They had to be reached down short flights of stairs because of the way the road fell off. The gully on that side of the road was overgrown with bananas and plantain. We passed a sign advertising a house for rent, which we inquired about. It rented for 8,000 CFAs a month—the same price we were paying daily at the Church Center. However, the woman that we had asked cautioned us that the ravine was an unhealthy place.

We came to a bar at the end of the street, where a few men sat around tables, drinking and watching TV. It was the nearest place to our apartment that sold cold beer. We turned right down a short street that dipped as it crossed a culvert for a trash-filled stream and then rose again to a busy commercial street that led left to the roundabout.

The street was lined on both sides with commercial establishments. Many years of rainy seasons had washed the dirt away from the left side of the road, which dropped off a foot or two, and any vehicle that went off the edge would risk severe structural damage. We watched many cabs come close to the edge, but didn't see any accidents. A gutter, two yards deep and a yard wide, ran along the other side of the road. A smaller gutter would not have accommodated the heavy rains of the rainy season.

There was a haze in the air, and the cliffs of Upper Station, two miles away from us, were barely visible. Just before the roundabout, we passed a huge, three-story building on the right. It had been the only building with lights the night we had arrived, and obviously had its own generator. A large sign on the front of the building identified it as Paul's Computer School.

The roundabout was a large traffic island at the junction of four streets that led off in various directions. A steady flow of traffic circulated around it. Commercial Avenue, the most prominent, was a broad avenue of three and four story buildings with stores at ground level. The Vatican Supermarket was on the ground floor of a three-story building, facing Commercial Ave. Next door, in the same building, was a restaurant where we decided to have lunch.

We pushed our way through a beaded curtain, and took one of the four tables outside the entrance. Persistent flies visited the sticky remnants of food left on the plastic placemats. Our waiter appeared, and wiped them ineffectually with a damp rag. He handed me a menu that was as limp as a badly worn dollar bill. There were seven or eight items listed, including bushmeat (which could have been hedgehog, rat, civet cat, or even monkey). We ordered Beef Ndole, which is beef in a sauce made with cashews or peanuts and vegetables, and french fries, which are served almost everywhere, and two bottles of "33". I have seldom had colder beer, but the Ndole tasted so strongly of fish that we thought that perhaps the waiter had gotten our order wrong, until we found the beef, and then some bones that I hoped were chicken. It was clear that nothing was wasted in that restaurant.

After lunch we shopped next door at the "Supermarket", which was a misleading name for a small store with only three short aisles containly the limited variety of groceries available. Local people did their shopping in the open markets, and had little use for food like canned tuna from Europe, at 1,500 CFAs per can, which was enough money to feed a large family for several days. Compared to an American store, it was chiefly notable for the absence of all dairy products or convenience foods. We later found most of what we bought that day for much less money in the open market: bottled water, toilet paper, soap, sugar cubes, instant coffee, etc. Two six-packs of two-liter bottles of water were heavy, so we took a share cab back to the Church Center.

Next morning we were the first people to appear at breakfast. Sunrise in our part of Cameroon was at 6:30 A.M. We showered and made our beds before we walked to the dining hall, which was separated from the Administration Building by a wide terrace of ornamental plants. The food was on the table when we arrived. There was a conference going on, and six long tables in the dining room had each been set for twenty people. There were some empty tables, but we saw a table with two place settings, and knew that we were expected. We found hot coffee in large thermos bottles, but platters of plain omelets were rapidly cooling. There were also platters with slabs of French bread, and we found little packages of butter from France. Apricot preserve was available as well as a tasty chocolate spread called Tartine, which I grew fond of. I didn't enjoy the cold plain omelet, and Lorna urged me to make my preference for hard-boiled eggs known to the cooks. I did that, and thereafter I had hard-boiled eggs every morning for breakfast, but so did everyone else. We had finished our breakfast by the time members of the Christian conference began filing in.

That day, we began what became our routine. I took an armchair to our enclosed porch where I wrote, while Lorna went off to draw. I might have dozed off for a moment, and when I looked up I saw a slender young man, dressed in a white shirt, sandals and dark trousers, sitting on the low wall at the front of our porch and looking at me with soft, dark eyes. He was sitting with one knee up, and seemed completely relaxed. "I am Noah", he announced. I welcomed him and introduced myself. He suggested he could be of help to us. If we went out at night, he could come along and be our bodyguard. I told him that might work, but first I wanted Lorna's ideas on the subject. We could talk another time. As he left, he told me he was cooking some beans, and would bring us some. When Lorna returned, I told her about Noah, and moments later, he reappeared, carrying a chipped enamel pot of red beans. The beans were delicious, and we often cooked them ourselves after we found where they were sold in the market.

We were awakened early Sunday morning by the sound of loud drumming. It was coming from the large field that separated our apartment from the entrance to the Church Center. We looked out and saw there were already several buses parked across the street, and the drumming was growing louder. Large groups of drummers were emerging from the buses and marching onto the field. Several hundred participants had already arrived. Signs on the buses indicated they were youth groups from all over Northwest Province. The women in each group wore uniforms of matching head and skirt wraps, and most of the men wore white shirts with black trousers. Most of them seemed to be young people, but there were some older people included as well.

Just outside our window, a group of men were assembling a large xylophone, with nearly a dozen bars of graduated length, which they laid in succession across a pair of freshly cut banana or plantain trunks. Several men played on it simultaneously, beating it with sticks to produce the tones for a line of young dancers, each of whom added his or her percussion to the rhythm with calf and ankle shakers or hand rattles.

The drums were of various types. The slit or talking drum was a large, hollowed-out log that was laid on its side and had a slit like a ballot box from which the deep, hollow sounds of the interior emerged. The tsombes were more conventional large drums, with deep tones, that contrasted with the sharp, tight tones of the smaller drums that the marchers carried. Each group that marched onto the field added a new flash of color to the wide expanse of red earth. They took their places in turn, along the benches that marked the perimeter. I immediately got my camera and began taking photographs. The drums of each arriving group added to the thunderous roar, which was to continue throughout the day. We watched two lines of dancers on our lawn engaging in a ritual combat consisting of advances and withdrawals. As one line turned their backs and stepped away, the other line would advance and symbolically smite them with fronds. I photographed groups all over the field, similarly engaged.

One of the many clergymen in attendance told me that there were more than fifteen hundred people on the field. The dances that the participants engaged in seemed to be an expression of the traditional animist beliefs of the area. I asked the clergyman how these practices could coexist with the modern Christian faiths of the performers. "It's very simple", he told me, "We have folk dancing groups just like many other countries do". I looked at the dancing groups dispersed on the field, and realized they were not dissimilar to dancers from the Gaspe Peninsula that I had watched when I was in Canada. The dancing went on all day. I took dozens of photographs while Lorna busily sketched. During the late afternoon, there was a competition in which judges chose the best groups. The day ended with a general dance in which all of the participants as well as many onlookers engaged. The dancers gaily circled the field three times in a great, counter-clockwise sweep. It was dusk when the celebration ended, and we walked back to our apartment.

It was getting quite dark by the time we cooked dinner and we were just sitting down to eat when Noah came in. We offered to share some of our dinner with him, but he had already eaten. He wanted to borrow our cell phone in order to get in touch with his father, who was a policeman in Wum. He promised to bring it right back, in fifteen minutes at most. We let him take it, and I left to buy some cold beer at a bar down the road. When I came back, Lorna and I played a game of Twenty Questions for a while. It was a good way to pass the time, since we sat in the dark so as not to attract insects.

Two hours passed. Noah had still not returned with our phone, and Lorna was getting worried about it. We had a general idea of where he lived, so we set off in the dark to find his house. At the place where we thought he lived, a young woman named Maribelle answered the door. When we explained our problem with Noah, she offered to call him on her cell phone if we would give her our cell number. When she reached him, she spoke to him sternly and he promised to bring back our phone immediately. He couldn't have been far, because he appeared almost as soon as we got back to our apartment, completely unabashed by his tardiness.

CH 12

Thievery and friendship

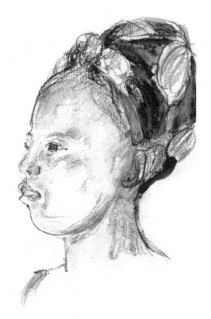

Maribelle

We were interested in the arts and crafts of Cameroon, which talented artisans were still producing by the methods of their ancestors. There was a large handicraft cooperative in Upper Station, and we planned to visit it the next day. There was a clinic across from our apartment, which served many of the medical needs of the community, and taxis were always available there. After breakfast, as we walked over to engage a taxi, I realized that Upperstation would be a great place to take pictures, and that I had forgotten to bring my camera. I asked Lorna to wait there while I ran back for it.

I kept it on top of my dresser, but when I looked for it, it wasn't there. Did I put it in a drawer? I looked through every drawer and couldn't find it. I started to ransack the entire room, in a rising tide of despair. I had to face the fact that it was gone again, after having retrieved it so miraculously in Garoua.

Lorna came back to see what was taking me so long. She reacted with her customary calm to what I had to tell her. We tried to piece together our actions the previous evening. Was there a chance that the camera had simply fallen out of my pocket? However, we couldn't overlook the possibility that Noah had taken it. The wonderful pictures I had taken the previous day were gone, and I felt our day had been spoiled too much to take the excursion we had planned.

That evening, we were just preparing to eat our dinner when Noah turned up again. I asked him how his day had gone, and he told me that it had gone well, and he inquired about my day. "I have had a terrible day", I told him. "I lost my camera, and it has ruined our entire trip. I must have dropped it out of my pocket on the way back from the field last night." Noah put on a suitably sympathetic expression.

"Someone might have found it," Lorna remarked and she asked Noah if he could spread the word around that it was missing.

"I would certainly be grateful to anyone who found it", I added. I told Noah that he could offer a reward of 10,000 CFAs ($20.00) for its recovery. Noah said that he might be able to help us and left to make some inquiries.

He returned twenty minutes later, along with a young man who had my camera in his hand. He told us that he had found it under a tree. I gave him the reward, but I also had to give Noah something for his assistance. When I checked my camera, I saw that the battery was dead, and it would have been worthless without a new battery or a battery charge. We knew of course that Noah had taken it. He came by after breakfast the next morning to tell us he was going to Wum to visit his father for a few days.

Our guidebook recommended a restaurant called Gracie's on Commercial Street, the wide avenue that ran south from the City Chemist's roundabout, and although it was a reasonably short walk, we were hungry, so we took a cab. We entered Gracie's through a beaded curtain, into a small interior with space for two tables, each with places for six or eight people. The menu was written on a chalkboard, and consisted of steak, eggs, salad, and French fries. We placed our orders with one of the cooks, who stood behind a counter that he could raise and lower like a train gate. He brought us cold beer immediately, and we joined the general conversation at the table, which consisted mostly of pleasantries. It was friendly, and we felt that we fit in.

The food was piled high on our plates. We each had slices of a thin steak, similar to a skirt steak, topping an enormous pile of somewhat limp French fries. I was concerned that they were probably cooked in palm oil. There was also a large salad of grated carrots, cabbage, and other leaves, and I wondered about the wisdom of eating it. We have always been told to be careful of fresh produce while traveling, so I only ate a small amount. When the feared consequences never materialized, I enjoyed all of the salads on subsequent visits. Large chunks of French bread accompanied our meal, and we resolved to look for a boulangerie so that we could enjoy it at home. The cost of our meal was 2,300 CFAs. That's less than $5.00 for two people. Gracie's became our favorite restaurant.

Next door to Gracie's was a Prescraft ('Protestant Crafts') Store, which we looked through after lunch. At the time that Cameroon achieved its independence in 1960, all emphasis was on the future, and there was danger that the ancient crafts would be lost. Weavers, woodworkers, metalworkers, and potters were turning away from the practice of their crafts because there was no market for their products.

In 1960, a Swiss minister by the name of Hans Knopfli founded the Protestant Handicrafts Center, which is now called Prescraft. He had trained as a cabinetmaker before his ordination, and joined the Basel Mission after studying theology in Basel and Oxford. He traveled to Cameroon for the first time in 1956, where he worked as a pastor and a manager of rural primary schools in Northwest Province. He began the enterprise called Prescraft in Bafut and Bali-Nonga, two towns near Bamenda, and he served as its full-time leader until 1982, when he handed the enterprise to J.K. Nyonka. He then launched the Protestant Pottery Project, now called Prespot, in Barmessing, where he continued to live for eleven more years before he returned to Switzerland.

The Prescraft Store sold native crafts that demonstrated many aspects of Cameroonian culture. There were musical instruments, carvings, woven goods, and bronze castings. They made wonderful sets of bronze chess pieces, with each warrior holding a spear or dagger, and the major pieces depicting royalty or their noble attendants. They cost about 40,000 CFAs per set ($80.00), and we would need to think about such a large expenditure. We bought a few small things for gifts.

On most days we worked after breakfast. Lorna usually went out to find a landscape or building that she could draw. The watercolor pencils that she bought for our trip worked well, and she needed to carry only a small bottle of water. She was filling her sketchbooks with wonderful pictures. In the outdoors, she always attracted an audience of children, usually schoolgirls in their blue uniform dresses with white collars, and she sometimes found it hard to work with their never-ending questions. She once tried to hide herself in a hedge and draw from there, but they found her almost immediately.

I liked to take an easy chair to one of our porches and enjoy the sun and the view while I wrote up my notes. From the long porch at the front of our building, I watched boys from a school at the top of a high, grassy hill performing calisthenics. They were far enough away that they seemed like ants against the sky. I too collected an audience of schoolchildren, until they lost interest in us after a few weeks.

We often picked up school papers that the children had dropped on our lawn, and we were impressed with the level of the education the children were getting. Fourth graders were performing the same arithmetical operations with Roman numerals that I had been taught at the same age. Their compositions seemed to be appropriate to their age levels.

Some of the workers at the Protestant Center took it upon themselves to supply Lorna with interesting items that she could draw, like enormous insects. Her most productive supplier was a gardener whom she called "my hero". It was also his job to announce breakfast every morning on the talking drum. She always had a coin for him when he proudly appeared with some great, wiggling bug between two fingertips.

The day after our first lunch at Gracie's, I found the location of the boulangerie. It was about a block beyond the City Chemist's roundabout and I walked there and back. There was a steady line of traffic, and I found the sidewalks thronged with people.

A day later, we decided to make a second attempt to visit to the Handicraft Cooperative on Upper Station. There were no taxis at the rotary near the clinic, so we walked towards Commercial Street to find one. Normally, by the time we reached it, several cabs would have passed going or coming from the Church Center, but we didn't find a taxi until we were in front of the 'George Bush Beauty Salon'. It was then that we learned that there was a one-day strike by the taxi owners to protest excessive police regulation. The only regulations we ever saw enforced were at checkpoints, at which every vehicle's window stickers and documents were carefully scrutinized. Woe, then, to any driver with an irregularity.

We found a taxi driver who offered to take us, for three times the usual fare, but since that only amounted to 900 CFAs (less than $2.00) we climbed in. There were many people walking, and many tried to flag down the cab, but our driver ignored them. He seemed to be driving a little fast, but traffic was light on account of the strike that we didn't get nervous until a group of pedestrians, more aggressive than most, stood in the road with their arms out to try to force us to stop. Our driver aimed the taxi directly at them and floored the accelerator. They barely escaped with their lives, and we realized our driver was not a sane person. This incident was repeated twice more before we reached our destination. The Handicrafts Center and its associated restaurant occupied a small group of buildings set on a leveled area at the edge of the escarpment, but we were now traveling so fast that we had turned into the next switchback before we could convince our driver to slow down enough to turn around.

He left us on the other side of the road in front of a woodcarver's shop, which we looked into first. There were about six men engaged in carving large doors with panels, in such high relief that they reminded me of Ghiberti's 'Doors of Paradise" at the Baptistry of the Cathedral in Florence. The work was so fine and detailed and the relief so high that in the United States there would be people who would want to design their houses around such doors.

We crossed the road to the Handicrafts Center, which was four times the size of the Prescraft Store on Commercial Street. I bought a carved walking stick there, for which I have since had compliments from everyone who sees it. There was a restaurant next door, which was built on the very edge of the escarpment, and we took seats at one of a line of round tables on a narrow balcony that projected over low, residential hills. There were a group of businessmen talking French at the next table. They were wearing fezzes, which we had never before seen in Cameroon, and we suspected that they might be Nigerian.

The browns and greens of the scene below us reminded me of a Cezanne painting. From our vantage point we could see people walking on the narrow paths to their houses. Many were heavily burdened, probably with supplies from the market, which was hidden two or three miles away in the haze.

The waiter had just brought our beer when my cell phone rang. It was Clara, and she was calling before she left school. We described our surroundings to her and got the latest news from home. Jeanne's pregnancy was proceeding on schedule, and everyone was well. It was far less expensive for Clara to call from the United States than for us to call her, and we talked for more than twenty minutes on Clara's five-dollar phone card.

Almost every day in Bamenda, we increased our circle of friends. Che Aaron had brought us a CD of his music, but we didn't have access to a player, and consequently couldn't listen to it at that time. Che dreamt of recognition and world acclaim, culminating, he hoped, with a triumphant tour of the United States. He wanted to believe that Lorna and I would be the vehicles for his success.

Lorna's son-in-law, Fung, worked as a DJ in a small venue, and we promised that we would bring Che's CD to Fung's attention. Every morning, before he began his day's work, Che stopped by our table for a few minutes, ate a slice of bread, and dreamt aloud about his future triumphs as a Rock Star. He invited us to lunch with him the following Sunday, when we could hear his music for ourselves. He knew that the manager of the restaurant we were going to owned a CD player. Lorna suggested that it might be fun if Patience came with us. She was the young woman who had met us on the night of our arrival.

Early one evening, just as it was getting dark, there was a knock on our door. When I answered it I found two young women standing there. They were looking for someone we didn't know, but we invited them in anyway. Their names were Germaine and Mercy, and they were both beautiful young women, elegantly turned out in their African dress. We offered them Cokes, and they introduced themselves. Germaine told us that she worked as an accountant at a small loan company downtown. Mercy, who seemed shyer, spoke with a rich contralto voice. She cared for four tenuously related children that had been passed along to her. They were intrigued to learn that Lorna was an artist, and before they left, they promised to return and sit for portraits.

Saturday morning, as we were beginning to go about our work for the day, a car stopped on the road that ran above our front door. It was the Director's wife, and she had come to invite us for lunch at her house. She told us that she had hoped to invite us earlier, but her husband, the Reverend Joseph, was recovering from a recent bout of malaria and had not been strong enough to receive visitors.

Her name was Jeanne, and we guessed that she was in her forties. She was an attractive woman, light skinned with reddish hair, and the slight excess of weight that was becoming to so many Cameroonian women. She had been informed that we were coming to stay at the Church Center by Fung's sister Cynthia in Buea, who was the wife of the Moderator, and she had been expecting us. The Director's house, like the Moderator's house in Buea, was at the rear of the Center at its highest point. It was a stone ranch, just beyond and slightly higher than the Business Manager's house. It was only a short walk from our apartment at the front of the center, but Cynthia came by in her car and drove us to her house for lunch. The Reverend Joseph seemed frail when we first met him; he still had fever blisters on his upper lip, and his voice was soft. He told us that he was recovering quickly, and would soon take us to Wum.

We lunched on chicken and cocoyams, a turnip-like tuber, and fried plantain. After lunch, Jeanne drove us to another part of Bamenda, where there was a charitable institution that she wanted us to see. It was called Aid International and we met its Director, who made a presentation to us about the problems it was created to address.

Cameroon is one of the countries where extreme poverty and misery resulted from the economic reforms (Economic Structural Adjustment Plan) mandated by the World Bank and IMF in the 1990s. Consequently, there had been an increasing number of orphans and street children because of the high death rate among parents that these reforms resulted in. This misery was exacerbated by deaths from AIDS, a cause not unrelated. By the World Bank's own estimate, 70% of the population lived under the poverty line.

Mercy, whom we had met the night before, and who cared for four orphans, was an example. Germaine told us that the toilet had fallen in at Mercy's house, and the power company, an American firm that was a subsidiary of Enron, had turned out her lights as well. The electric rates were the most expensive item in most families' budgets.

Cameroon had recently privatized its power grid. Lorna and I referred Mercy to the Aid International Director for help. Aid International also helps widows, who are severely disadvantaged in Cameroon by the traditional, hereditary rules. If a woman becomes a widow, her brother-in-law inherits the family's property, and many widows are put out in the street with their children when an unkind brother-in-law takes possession. The Director showed us the books of the organization, and we were impressed that even a gift as small as a book or a piece of cloth was duly recorded and accounted for, that it was run by volunteers, and that unlike most charities, 100% of the contributions were used for their intended purposes.

When Che Aaron arrived with Patience on Sunday morning to take us to the restaurant for lunch, he was dressed in an elegant white costume, and he smiled with pleasure when we told him how handsome he looked. Patience also looked very attractive, in a long belted dress that emphasized her small waist. Short puffed sleeves and a deeply cut square neck displayed her fine collarbones to advantage. Patience smiled readily, but sometimes her smile changed almost imperceptibly to an uncertainty that betrayed self-consciousness or vulnerability. We engaged a taxi at the rotary in front of the clinic to take us to the restaurant.

It was called 'The Businessman's Restaurant', and was owned by an Arabic man who was Che's friend. He showed us to a long, narrow room on the second floor, where we all took seats in a row, looking out toward Sonac Street. Lorna tried to see to it that Patience and Che sat together, but Che announced (rather gratuitously and meanly I thought) that she was not his girlfriend. Patience looked wounded for a moment, and then passed it off.

Che ordered for everybody, and the owner brought in a CD player so that we could play Che's music. Several of his songs dealt with AIDS, and were played in rock style. Che had hoped that the government would use his music in its AIDS awareness campaign, but his songs were in English, which was spoken only in two provinces, and most of the advertising that we saw was in French, and addressed SIDA, the French acronym for the disease.

Che ordered *achoo*, a quintessential Cameroonian comfort food, for everyone. We had watched Nia and Dabala eat it in Maroua, but Lorna and I had never tried it. The waitress spooned what looked like cream of wheat into our bowls, and made cavities in the center of our bowls with her ladle, into which she poured a scoop of yellow, oily liquid with a large curlicue of roasted skin. Our readiness to eat it in the Cameroonian fashion, with the first two fingers of our right hands, seemed to raise our status. We had successfully passed a test! A bowl of water was ceremoniously passed around before and after our meal, and as we relaxed with our beer, we enjoyed the sense of bonding that we felt.

Patience left us after lunch, and Che took us to see his house, which was a short walk up a gully behind the restaurant. We met Che's father, who was drinking with some friends at a bar, and we stopped for a visit at Che's house. It was a small cottage with tiny rooms. We sat at the kitchen table, and Che served us some palm wine and showed us his diplomas from school, and clippings from the local newspaper that recognized his musical compositions.

Che lived on the same hill as the Protestant Center, and we walked home along a path that followed the crest. It seemed shorter than the taxi ride to the restaurant. There were houses along the route, and some gullies with dense vegetation, which Lorna planned to return to with her sketchbook.

CH 13

Paul's Computer School

Noah

The following week started badly. I was catching a cold and resting on my bed while Lorna went off to draw. We hadn't seen Noah since he left for Wum, but he appeared at our door shortly after Lorna left. From the way he wandered around our apartment after I had let him in, it seemed, I thought, that he was determined to steal something. I was worried about money that I kept in a drawer, as well as a camera, binoculars, and other valuable things that were on top of a dresser.

I knew that Lorna kept money in a drawer in her wardrobe, and I wanted to keep him away from her side of the room as well.

I didn't give any thought to our cell phone, which lay beside me on the bed in a welter of papers and notebooks. He asked to borrow a pen and notebook, and I passed him one that was beside me on the bed. He wrote a page about how much he disliked Wum, which didn't seem relevant to anything. I thought it was probably an attempt to distract me. He asked for water, and rather than leave him alone, I sent him to the kitchen to get his own water.

Every time he moved to Lorna's side of the room, I jumped up and went with him, and when he walked to my dresser, I did the same. I was relieved when he left. I thought that he had left in frustration and I closed the doors and returned to my nap. When Lorna came in, we made dinner and prepared to wind up our day.

We had bought a cell phone card, and were planning to call Jeanne and Clara and one of my sisters, but when I looked for the card, it was gone from the spot where I had left it. A moment later, I really panicked when I looked for our cell phone. Noah had succeeded.

That night, we tried all the things we had done the night that Noah had borrowed our phone. We walked the narrow paths to Noah's house in pitch-blackness, and told his friends and relations our story. No one could reach him. I tried calling our own number on a cell phone I borrowed from the night guard at the Center. Someone answered, but refused to respond further, and must have shut the phone off after that, because it kept ringing on subsequent calls. Lorna was distressed at being cut off from talking with her daughter, but we were still hopeful that we might recover our phone, as we had my camera.

Noah had heard we were trying to reach him, and came by the next morning after breakfast. I tried the reward routine again, but this time he wasn't buying. When I accused him outright of having taken it, he calmly pointed out that our doors were always wide open, and anyone could slip in quickly and steal from us. I was unable to say with certainty that that wasn't what had happened.

Noah continued to visit us frequently, as if nothing had happened between us, and Lorna and I found it impossible to dislike him for what had resulted from my own carelessness. Cameroon is a poor country, and Noah didn't have a job. People do what they must to survive.

Our social circle was expanding daily. Germaine brought her mother, whose name was Elizabeth, to visit. Elizabeth was a strong and vital woman in her forties, with a ready laugh, who always wore a white short-sleeved blouse with her matching headcloth and wraparound skirt. When she saw the drawings that Lorna was making, she took it upon herself to be the supplier of native plants for Lorna to draw.

Sometimes we would hear her calling 'Lorna, Lorna", at first light, before we were even up, and we would put something on and find her on our little enclosed porch with some huge plant, once even a whole tree that she had carried for two miles over steep tracks. She walked with a long step, and seemed to cover ground effortlessly.

Germaine told us that she had a sister, Cynthia, who was majoring in zoology at the university in Dschang. Dschang is a city about two hours from Bamenda. Germaine told us that Cynthia was very black, but it was a purely descriptive statement, devoid of any overtones of judgment. When I met Cynthia, I liked her at once. She was a consummate coed, and she looked very chic in a black leather jacket.

Elizabeth and her daughter often came in the evening, bringing dinner for us all. We tried to keep a good supply of beer and Coke on hand, as well as grenadine for Cynthia, who liked it especially. We often sat and talked as late as 10:00 P.M. Nights when we were alone, we settled in to our respective cots right after dinner, because our lights were too dim to read by. We usually played Twenty Questions until we fell asleep.

Light attracts insects, and the mosquitos began coming for us as soon as the sun went down. They were followed by other insects, including moths, some of which rivalled small birds in size. Lorna captured some of them with her collection kit, and made beautiful, delicate drawings of them.

As for the mosquitos, we took our doxycycline pills daily. Noah told us that people burned something called 'Moon Tiger' to keep mosquitos away. It was a slow-burning coil (one coil lasted an entire night) that was mounted on a pointed support. It produced an acrid smoke that kept most of the mosquitos away. It irritated our lungs as well, and we suspected that longtime usage would not be good for us. The alternative was to close all the doors and windows and spray our rooms nightly, but we enjoyed the night air and preferred to leave our porch doors open.

Often, late at night, the guard making his rounds flashed his light into our room, and I think he felt we were remiss in not locking up. It was cold in the early hours of the morning, and most nights Lorna crawled into my narrow cot where we finished the night nested like a pair of spoons.

Lorna was unhappy with the possibility that one of her daughters could telephone, and we would not be able to receive her call. We needed to replace our phone. It cost ninety dollars, and it made us more careful with our possessions. Word of our loss had spread among the workers at the Center, and they were outraged, and hostile toward Noah when he came around. The guard seized him one morning as he was coming for a visit, and we needed to intercede for his release.

In the spirit of restitution, Noah offered to introduce me to Paul, who founded the computer school we so often passed on our way downtown. I thought it would be interesting, and made an appointment to go with him later in the week.

A large group of people from North America came to stay at the Center for a few days. They arrived in a collection of small buses and vans, and filled all the other guesthouses, which included a dormitory in one building, and several individual rooms in others. Some were single people, but there were several families with young children and two with tiny babies. They belonged to an organization for the preservation of languages, and they were about to disperse into various communities among natives of particular groups, in order to produce dictionaries, grammars, and eventually a translation of the Bible.

Walking back from breakfast one morning, we saw two vehicles that had arrived during the night parked at the top of the hill. They had set up tents, and I could see four people busy preparing breakfast. One vehicle was a land cruiser, and the other looked like an old-fashioned trailer with rounded edges, which, however, was self-propelled, and I learned that it had been manufactured in Austria.

An hour later, I walked up to their site. There was only a young French woman there. She was blonde and attractive and didn't speak much English. We spoke French, and she told me that she and her companion, an Austrian, had met a British couple in Niger who shared their destination, which was South Africa. They had all decided to travel together. Lorna and I met the other members of their party a little later, when they showered in our guesthouse. The shower room was next to our apartment, and we talked to them frequently in the two days that they stayed at the Center. They traveled with a large Bernese mountain dog that liked to lie on the wet floor of the shower room. They are about the size of German Shepherds but have long hair with characteristic patches of three colors, like money cats. They are very sweet tempered, and three young boys who passed on their way to school fell in love with him. Dogs are scarce in Cameroon, and a dog like this was very unusual.

Lorna and I spoke with the boys, who were shy and hung back, but the smallest one, who was more forthcoming, told us that his name was Menard. They seemed to be about twelve years of age, and Menard was very interested in Lorna's drawings. He told Lorna that he drew a lot himself, and she asked him if he would sit for a portrait, and he agreed.

Menard was a bright young man, and he began visiting us frequently on his way home from school. I was usually at home writing up my notes while Lorna was out drawing somewhere, so Menard and I would chat for an hour or so. He was good in school, and enjoyed writing rap lyrics as well as drawing.

He invited us to watch his soccer team play in a match on Saturday, and Lorna and I attended the game. It was held on the large field near the entrance of the Center, and we could see that Menard, besides being the coach and manager of his team, was also the star player. He seemed to get the ball often and send it where he wanted. Unfortunately, the game had to end when their soccer ball broke.

I bought a deck of cards and played '500 Rummy' as a respite from '20 Questions'. I taught Menard to play, and we often played until Lorna came back from drawing. Menard also came to sit for some portraits. He didn't want to take any pay from Lorna because he considered her to be a friend, and he felt that one shouldn't take money from friends. Lorna convinced him that he should receive the same pay that she gave to other friends who brought her material to draw.

Noah came at 10:00 on Friday morning to take me to meet Paul, who ran his eponymously named school near the Chemist's Roundabout. Paul was at his desk in a small office. We were shown in at once by a woman who seemed to be his assistant. Unlike most African women, she wore Western business attire. Paul stood up and shook my hand, and nodded at Noah, who took a straight chair by the door while I took an armchair beside his desk. Paul swiveled his chair to face me and leaned back. He was a lanky Midwesterner, with gray hair and still-youthful features. I had been curious about his school since the night we had initially driven into Bamenda. The darkness had been total, with the exception of the school, which was the only building with lights.

Paul told me that his computers needed a reliable power supply to avoid problems, and that he had installed his own generators. When he had first come to Bamenda as a Peace Corps volunteer in 1992, he had been assigned to teach at the Allo School that occupied a hilltop next to the Protestant Center. It was a period of great political turmoil; elections were taking place, and the candidate contesting Paul Biya, the President, was the Anglophone leader of the Social Democrats, John Ndi Fruh, a native of Bamenda.

I had heard about the turmoil of the period from Nia, who had been driving a taxi at that time. Bamenda had then been a hotbed of anti-government unrest, and raging mobs had killed many people by burning rubber tires around their necks. I had read back issues of the local papers that were stored in the library of the Center and learned that as high an official as the chief judge of Bamenda Court had been murdered, and dumped in a ditch along Sonac Street.

Paul was living, at that time, in a small house on the school grounds that was supplied to him by the school administration, which had close ties to the government in power. He was awakened one morning by the sound of many voices and when he went out to his small porch, he saw that a large crowd had a gathered in front of his house. When he appeared, a cry immediately went up: "Burn him! Burn him!" He thought at that moment that his life was over, but a young woman came out of the crowd and stood in front of him. She turned to the crowd and shouted "Nobody touch this man!" His house was burned, but he found out later that there had been some wellwishers in the crowd who had been able to rescue some of his belongings from the destruction.

Paul, whose last name was Mickelson, was a Beloit, Wisconsin firefighter, who after twenty-seven years with the Beloit Fire Department had taken early retirement in 1992 and joined the Peace Corps. In 1997 he sold his house in Wisconsin, withdrew his pension and founded 'Paul's Computer Institute' with an original staff of three, and fifteen students. His current staff numbered thirty all Cameroonian, and the student body had grown to four hundred. We toured the building, a three-story structure, and I saw classroom after classroom of students engaged in repairing hardware, writing code, or manipulating data in some way. Noah tagged along with us, obviously proud that he had introduced me to this man.

Paul lived in Upper Station, and invited me to his house. He told me that he no longer brought many people to his home, because things would often go missing, and I wondered if his rather pointed remark was meant for Noah. I made an appointment to visit him again along with Lorna, which we did a few days later. We never had the opportunity to visit him at his home, because he left for his annual visit to the U.S. a week later. These trips were important means of obtaining funds and other resources for the school. Two or three of the school's Cameroonian administrators usually came along with him on his trips to the United States.

There was a great deal of support in the greater Beloit area for his school, and Paul had been honored for his work in Cameroon with the President's Medal at the 2001 commencement at Beloit College. It had only been bestowed on two prior occasions. Rotary International had also been an important source of support for his school. On his last visit to the United States he had been able to fill a large shipping container with computers and books that he had shipped to Douala for $5,900.00. It had then cost him a further $5,000.00 to ship the container the final two hundred miles to Bamenda. Paul told me that he knew our friend Germaine very well. She had been a scholarship student at the school, and had worked there briefly.

Most of the new people we met in Bamenda had some connection with those we already knew. There was a large gas station that we cut through just before the Prescraft store. While we were cutting through it on our way to the store, a man filling his car's gas tank spoke to me. I stopped, while Lorna went on ahead, and we talked at length. He was the husband of the Prescraft bookkeeper whom we had already met. He was also an old friend of Elizabeth, Germaine's mother. His name was Mr. Patrick, and his job required him to live in Douala, apart from his wife, and he was filling his gas tank to return there. During our conversation, I told him that we were returning to the U.S. in about a month, so that we would be on hand for the birth of Jeanne's twins.

He told me that to be the parents of twins in Cameroon was an honor greater than any other honor or degree that society can bestow. The mother of a twin is henceforth addressed by the title Manyi, and the father will forever after be called Tanyi. He, himself, was a parent of twins, and I felt that even as a prospective grandparent (when Lorna and I are married) I had gained his immediate respect.

The rituals surrounding the birth of twins in the Western Grasslands are elaborate. They are regarded as godlike children, and any twins born in a Fondom had to be reported to the Fon, who then sent a gift of palm oil and salt to the parents. There was a plant called the 'peace plant', which has deep green lanceolate leaves that plays an important role with regard to twins. Community leaders attach stems of the plant to the doorposts as a sign that the house contains twins. Germaine's mother Elizabeth brought stems of the "peace plant" for Lorna to draw, and she made some lovely colored drawings for her sketchbooks. The 'peace plant' is a member of the Dracaena family, and exists in two varieties, which seems to explain its choice as a symbol of twins. One might think that one plant represented a male and the other a female, but there was no general agreement about which of the two was which.

Reverend Joseph, the Director of the Center, was ready to take us to Wum. He had made a remarkable recovery from his malaria relapse; all signs of fragility and weakness had disappeared, and he looked to us like a vital and youthful man in his late forties. Our trip would take place the following Monday, and we promised to be ready to go by 6:00 AM.

CH 14

The Fondom of Bafut

Che Aaron

Che Aaron Maryo had continued stopping daily at the dining hall during our breakfast every morning. We hadn't been out together since our lunch at the Businessman's Restaurant, but now Che wanted to take us to visit the Fondom of Bafut, which was fifteen miles north of Bamenda on the Ring Road.

Bafut was made famous in several books written by Gerald Durrell, a former director of the London Zoo, in the late forties. They included *The Bafut Beagles* and *The Zoo in my Luggage*, in which he discussed the extensive assistance he received from the renowned Fon of Bafut.

Bafut, Che informed us with pride, was his home village. He had friends at the palace, and thought that perhaps he could arrange an audience with the Fon for us. Bafut was one of the most important Fondoms of the Western Grasslands. One intuitively thinks of grasslands as treeless plains, but this part of Cameroon had densely-forested hills and valleys, and many of the hills would certainly qualify as mountains in most localities. We made plans to meet Che on Sunday morning, and we invited a new friend, who had recently arrived at the Center, to come along with us.

This was Phil Wozencraft, an Englishman from Gloucester, who was traveling solo through Africa as far as his money would take him. When we first met Phil, he looked like Saddam Hussein emerging from his spider hole, but he got a haircut and trimmed his beard the next day.

His capacity for beer was enormous, and for the few days he was in Bamenda, I did my best to match him, usually drinking three or four quarts in an evening. Lorna was never able to keep up. There was a restaurant we liked on Commercial Avenue, which was at the top of Bamenda's version of the Spanish Steps of Rome. We enjoyed dining there al fresco, while darkness fell and Phil entertained us with his adventures. We watched the changing activity on the street below as people headed home. The buildings across from us were mostly three stories, with restaurants and shops on the first floor, and narrow metal balconies along the front of the second floor. Behind them, we could see the headlights of cars navigating the switchbacks on the road down from Upper Station. Our friend Germaine, who worked for a moneylender across the street, often joined us after work.

Phil told us about crossing Mali in three days on the back of an open truck which broke down in a tiny village, where he had to spend a week, and about escaping from a gang in the backstreets of Dakar who were trying to rob him, kidnap him, or worse. Phil usually worked at something in England until he had saved 10,000 pounds, which would enable him to travel for an extended period. He had previously traveled in Asia and the Americas, but this was his first trip to Africa. He passed along a book to me that he he had just finished, about a recreation of Captain Cook's voyage called *Blue Latitudes*, by Tony Horwitz. Besides traveling, he obviously enjoyed reading about it.

For our visit to Bafut, Lorna and I bought the customary bottle of French wine to present to the Fon in the event that we could get an audience. Fons in Cameroon have royal status, and consequently, they are entitled to obeisance from all. Even the President of the Republic recognizes their status, and accords them the traditional prerequisites of royalty. Fons are the supreme arbiters of any matter of the sort that would, in the United States, go for resolution to a Family or Probate Court. Some Fons even maintain their own prisons.

Sunday morning, everyone gathered at our apartment. When Che arrived he was wearing a matching blue outfit, heavily embroidered with orange thread, and he looked as resplendent as a Fon. Che was a bit of a peacock and he must have had a large wardrobe for he wore different clothing every time we had a special occasion. He brought along a young woman who was a backup singer in his group, and who had one of the loveliest slender figures I have ever seen. I could have encircled her waist with either arm, and did so when we took some photographs, prior to leaving.

We set out for a motorpark on the other side of town. At the front of the Church Center, instead of turning left toward the business center as usual, we went straight, which took us along a long, unpaved residential street. We stopped at a church, where Che was able to change our large bills into the more convenient small money, and then we continued for another mile.

We passed a barbershop that had an interesting handmade sign, and I took a picture of it. I hadn't noticed the man standing behind me, who was the owner. He approached me angrily, asserting that I had infringed on his property rights, and demanded payment. I tried to ignore him and walk on, but he followed me, protesting loudly. Lorna finally mollified him. She told him I would ask his permission, and pay money the next time, and that seemed to satisfy him.

At the motorpark, Che negotiated a ride to Bafut for the five of us, and we all piled into a share cab for the eight-mile trip. There were few cars on the road, which was an unmarked strip of macadam, wide enough for two lanes in each direction. We were stopped once at a checkpoint, while the driver's paperwork was inspected, but we were waved through two other checkpoints without stopping.

Bafut was at the left of a fork in the road that led to Wum. There was an intersection, with a church and a few stores, and a short street at the left that led into the palace grounds. We stopped for beer at a bar on the corner of the street, where we met Che's friend, who was a palace functionary. He collected the required payment and explained the ground rules for our visit.

We began our visit to the palace with a stop at the home of the queen. She was a large, impressive woman, massive with an upright carriage and a regal bearing, who seemed to float like an oceanliner as she walked. Lorna and I were not allowed to present our gift directly to her, but it was passed to her through a suitable intermediary. The queen herself, however, led our tour.

The palace buildings were dispersed over several acres. As we passed through various buildings, we kept catching glimpses of a mysterious and immense building with a grass roof that was hidden behind a fifteen-foot stockade fence. It reminded me of the building in 'King Kong' where the giant ape was found. When we finally entered the courtyard where it stood, we saw how impressive it really was. It had been built as a suitable abode for the spirits of the Fon's ancestors. The building had been erected on a platform that was six feet high, and consisted of lines of carved, vertically placed, massive logs, which soared to the proportionately massive grass roof. We were not able to meet the Fon, who was away from the palace, and we were also disappointed that his museum was closed.

It was late afternoon when we got back to Bamenda. We made a supper of piles of French fries and beer at Frimans, a basement restaurant on Commercial Street. Che left us there, and we walked home in the dark with our English friend who decided to leave us for a nightcap at the last bar that we passed.

CH 15

We finally get to Wum

We left for Wum Sunday morning before sunrise. We told the cook at the dining hall that we would miss breakfast, and we boiled some eggs in our own kitchen. Lorna was showering while the eggs were cooking, and just then, our phone rang. It was Jeanne calling from Truro, MA, and she was excited about a great opportunity to rent the large house next door to her for the entire summer season running from May through September. Owners of Cape properties can make a great deal of money, if they can find cheap accommodations for themselves, and rent out their properties during vacation times. During the previous year, Jeanne and Conrad periodically rented a nearby one-room cabin while renting out their own property for $3,500.00 a week. With twins arriving in June, it would be difficult to repeat this.

However, their neighbor had offered them his large house for $4,000.00 for the entire season, and Jeanne wanted to know if Lorna and I would consider sharing the expense with them, and spend the upcoming summer in Truro. Lorna came out of the shower and I passed her the phone so she could hear the proposition firsthand.

Jeanne had told me that her neighbor needed an answer in a few days. I thought that Lorna and I could discuss it, and then perhaps we could call Jeanne back with our decision, but the phone network in Cameroon is not always reliable, and we were afraid we might not be able to get back to her in time. Therefore, we made our decision before we hung up, and told Jeanne to accept for us.

A few minutes later, Reverend Joseph came by, driving a Toyota 4x4, in which we set off for Wum. Wum was about fifty miles north of Bamenda, on the northernmost section of the Ring Road, which we picked up at the same motorpark where we had employed the taxi to Bafut the previous day. After filling the gas tank at the motorpark, Reverend Joseph picked up our driver, who lived nearby.

The first seven or eight miles were familiar from the previous day, but at Bafut the road branched north through hilly country, where there were only scattered houses. The road was narrow, like a country road in the United States, and we kept to a moderate speed. The morning sun was softened by the early mist, which still lay over most of the land. Enroute, we passed Mentchum Falls, which were not readily visible from the road. Reverend Joseph ordered our driver to stop so we could take some pictures. At this time of year the flow was greatly reduced in volume, to only the equivalent of a large water main break. Nevertheless, the force of the flow was enough to propel the water in a long, sweeping arc into the gorge below.

As we resumed our ride, the road changed from pavement to red dirt, and continued that way for several miles before it changed back to pavement just before Wum. As we entered Wum, it felt like we were entering a quintessential frontier town in a Western movie. It was dry and flat, with a few low buildings set back from a dusty main street. There were few vehicles to be seen, and the few people abouwalked in the middle of the street.

We saw a rather short man wearing a straw 'coolie' hat carrying a pole, perhaps twenty feet in length, the two ends of which almost reached the ground. I wanted to photograph him, but I was too slow with my camera. We were to meet him again under very different circumstances in a few hours. I scanned our guidebook while Lorna went into a large native market with Reverend Joseph to buy the wine that would serve as the customary gift to the royalty that we planned to meet. Although Wum had a population of 51,744 according to our guidebooks, its downtown seemed to consist of only a few blocks of single homes, constructed in the local fashion of sun dried bricks, with low broad roofs, and no basements. The remainder of the population must have been widely spread.

While Lorna and Reverend Joseph were shopping, a few curious passersby stopped at the car to find out why we were in Wum. One was a Pentecostal minister, and it seemed very important to him to write his name in my notebook. When they returned from shopping, we drove to the house of Reverend Manfred, a senior minister in the area, who would stay with us during our visit. He lived in a modern, ranch-type house not far from where Reverend Joseph was having his own house built. We had seen many houses being built in Cameroon, and found the pace was usually glacial, often, we were told, lasting over a few years.

Reverend Manfred was a large man who wore a sky blue caftan and a white fez that I had thought only Nigerians wore. He greeted us and made a joking reference about Reverend Joe, who he informed us was his boss. We met his wife, a strong, attractive woman who was busy washing the floor. We would meet her later in the day at a function in celebration of Women's Day. Women's Day is an annual international holiday that recognizes the importance of women in society, and most of the women we met that day wore a commemorative printed cloth that had been specifically manufactured for the celebration. Even later in the day, as we drove back to Bamenda, we passed several bars still filled with women, singing and behaving slightly rowdy, in place of the men who usually filled the establishments.

With Reverend Manfred added to our entourage, we went first to the home of the village chief, to present him with our gift, and to receive his permission to visit the places we wished to see in Wum.

Surprisingly, he was the same little man we had seen, carrying the long pole down the street as we arrived. He received us, in his ceremonial robes, and custom required us to present our traditional gift to him through his assistant. We wanted to visit the Luke Memorial Church, which was under construction, since it honored Fung's father, who had been the first Moderator of the Protestant Church in Cameroon. We also wished to visit his gravesite at the palace, and meet with the dowager queen and her entourage. We received his permission.

We drove up a steep, deeply rutted gully that led to the top of the highest hill in the vicinity, where the church was being built. Construction was nearly complete: it needed only the addition of a roof, but it was already an active parish. We met the young minister assigned to it, and he told us that so many people had joined the parish since its inception that he needed a larger church, and he was thinking of moving its front wall outward before adding the roof.

We next drove to the palace, where construction was also taking place. The Fon, whom we had met at Clara's wedding, had still not returned from America. We visited the burial place of Fung's father, who was interred in a traditional niche grave at the side of one of the old palace buildings, which would place him actually under the building. In this way, his spirit could inhabit the building.

Almost twenty years prior to our visit, there had been a major disaster near Wum. On August 21st 1986, a landslide disturbed the deep layers of water in Lake Nyos, a nearby volcanic lake. As a result, an estimated 13 billion cubic yards of carbon dioxide bubbled to the surface and rolled across the surrounding countryside. It suffocated nearly 1,000 people, 3,000 cattle, and every other living thing in the vicinity. Wum, twenty miles away, became the center of the relief efforts that the world mounted to help the survivors.

I remembered reading the story of a young woman named Mercy, who survived because her family had sent her to Wum with a sum of money to buy provisions, and when she heard of the fate that had overtaken them, used the money to open a restaurant in Wum. I asked Reverend Manfred if he knew of her, and whether or not the restaurant was still in existence. He knew her well, and decided to bring us there for lunch. He telephoned her at once on his cell phone, and ordered lunch for the three of us plus our driver.

There was nothing to distinguish Mercy's house as a restaurant from any of the other houses on her street. She showed us into a large sitting room that was comfortably cool after the heat that had followed the early morning haze. A tall thin man was washing the stone floor when we entered, and he was still at it nearly an hour later when we left. Although eighteen years had passed since the tragedy that took her family, Mercy was still a youthful and capable-looking woman. She brought us cold beer to drink while we were waiting for the chicken and pepper soup that Reverend Manfred had ordered. He told us that it was his duty to play host when his boss came into town. We were served at the armchairs in which we were sitting, rather than at a table. The cold beer was a welcome accompaniment to the spicy pepper soup. After lunch we drove out to Lake Wum. It was in an area of low, treeless, grassy hills. Along the road, we passed a Fulani, herding a line of long-horned cattle.

Reverend Manfred dreamt that he would someday build a resort at the lake. Like Lake Nyos, Wum was a volcanic lake, very deep, and subject to the same kinds of disturbances. The pressure in the depths held massive amounts of carbon dioxide that could be set free like a shaken soda bottle if disturbed. Fortunately, Lake Wum had a more stable shoreline than Lake Nyos.

The Women's Day celebration was scheduled to begin in town at two o'clock. We drove to the large, communal hall, where nearly two hundred people, mostly women, had gathered. Many of the women were dressed in a cloth that had been specifically designed for the occasion. This was the day when women took the lead. Reverend Joseph was waiting for us there, and he introduced us to some of the more distinguished guests. Among them, we met an older woman, who had been the first female Member of Parliament for the district. A large buffet meal had been set up in the center of the room. Everyone sat on the perimeter, although at one end of the room there were a few rows of seats. We thought we were the only Westerners in the area, and we were surprised to see a young blond woman, seated fairly close to us. She turned out to be a Peace Corps worker who had been assigned to teach biology in Wum for a two-year period.

She lived with a local family, and was feeling a little lonely and homesick. She knew Brian, the young man from the Peace Corps that we had met on our way back from the far north. We joined the buffet line along with a group of the people with whom we had been sitting. Judging by their corner-of-the-eye appraisals, they seemed to be interested in how receptive we were to Cameroonian food. We had been in Cameroon long enough to readily pass the test, but I skipped the fish heads, which were piled high on a huge platter.

There was a young man who worked for the Institute for the Preservation of the Aghem Language, who wanted to go to Bamenda. Reverend Joseph agreed to bring him along, and I tried to encourage him to talk about his work at the Institute. He seemed shy, however, and his answers were not especially enlightening.

Food was cheaper in Wum than in Bamenda, and Reverend Joseph, engaging in the kind of arbitrage that travelers in Cameroon practice, directed our driver to stop at a few roadside stands, where he bought fifty-pound bags of various vegetables. At one stop, an entrepreneur held a dead civet cat in my face, which he hoped would tempt me into buying it for my dinner. At another stop, a car drew alongside us, whose occupants Reverend Joseph knew. It was a brown 1984 Toyota, which I mention only because it has a role later in this account. We didn't meet the driver at that time, since he stayed in his car, but we learned that he was Fung's nephew, Robert Graham Luke, who was driving his mother, Claudette, home to Douala.

Claudette came over to our vehicle and chatted with us briefly. She had been married to Fung's eldest brother Thomas, who had died under mysterious circumstances, shortly after he returned to Cameroon after a long visit to the United States. He had studied in the U.S. for eight years, and had majored in Accounting. He had returned to Cameroon when his father had been killed in an automobile accident.

Thomas, as the eldest brother was now the head of the large extended family and it became his responsibility to administer the property that his father had owned. Unfortunately, he died within a year. The cause was never clear and as in so many families, the estate became a matter of contention. And there were people who felt they had been shortchanged in the process.

Following his death, his mother fled to the United States with younger members of the family, including Fung, the youngest child.

This was necessary to avoid the possibility of an unwanted marriage, dictated by tradition.

After briefly chatting with Claudette, we drove on without then meeting her son Robert Graham Luke. We got back to Bamenda before nightfall, and Reverend Joseph shared some of the food he had bought with us as he dropped us off: lots of peanuts, mangos, and some pineapples.

CH 16

"Kidnapped"

We were staying in Bamenda for longer than we had expected; already we had extended our stay at the Protestant Center twice. Dabala, our tour director in the North, had found reasonable accommodations for us in Foumban, an important Fondom about a hundred miles away, on the far side of the Ring Road. However, when he telephoned us to confirm, we couldn't leave Bamenda because we had just scheduled our trip to Wum with Reverend Joseph.

Now we heard from Elsa that Fung's sister Claudia was coming to visit from America in two weeks, and that they would arrive in Bamenda on their way to visit their father's grave in Wum two days later. Lorna was nearly out of Commit pills and was in danger of reverting to cigarette smoking without them. We tried buying them from a pharmacy on Commercial Street, but their wholesaler was unable to obtain them in Cameroon.

With Claudia coming, however, there was a chance of a refill from America. Lorna telephoned Clara to buy some, and send it along with Claudia, which she promised to do. Now, I had to see the business manager to extend our stay for a third time. He drove a newish Toyota SUV, which he parked next to the Administration Building every day after driving it the few hundred yards down the hill from where he lived next to Reverend Joseph.

We passed it every morning on our way back from breakfast, but on the day I went to talk with him, I noticed there was a photograph of a young woman in the middle of the passenger's side of his windshield. When I asked him about it, he told me it was a picture of his sister-in-law, who had just died, and that it was their custom to display photos of lost loved ones in this manner. We were sorry to hear of his loss.

However, there was a slight problem with extending our stay; our quarters had been promised to members of a large religious conference that was to run for five days, but we could be accommodated in another space for the duration, and move back to our apartment when the conference ended. We would not need to move, however, until the end of the week.

That night, we heard what we learned was funeral music, and we wondered if it was perhaps for the business director's sister-in-law. We had heard it a few times before, been curious, and asked Che about it. It sounded like a short polka, played over and over again all night long, and whenever we heard it, we knew someone had died.

Almost every day, Lorna and I walked downtown. We bought most of our food at the large native market that occupied several acres behind the commercial buildings on the side of Commercial Street that got the sun in the morning. One entered just beyond Prescraft, where a line of dealers in fresh fruit and vegetables displayed their products. Another line of dealers on their right sold every kind of dried grain or milled product, from little cell-like stores that they could secure at the close of the day's business.

The rest of the market, spread across several acres, was taken up by lines of stores, each the size of a small room, which were roughly segregated by the kinds of merchandise they sold. Most of the stands at the front of the market sold general merchandise, which was replicated with little change at each booth. There we found most of the staples that we needed to buy often: bottled water, instant coffee, sugar, and toilet paper.

On our first visit to the market, we encountered a very pleasant woman who sold most of the things we needed, with the exception of bottled water. However she left us at her stand and disappeared into the market for five minutes, and when she returned, she was carrying a six-pack of the two-liter bottles that water is commonly sold in. She didn't add anything to the price for her efforts, but after that we always shopped with the same woman, and of course we always added something for her kindness.

Commercial Street had several banks, where we often changed our currency into the small denominations that we couldn't find anywhere else. Perhaps unsurprisingly, the guards in the banks wore Wakenhut patches on their uniforms, showing that they worked for the international company that is known for operating the prison system in Texas.

Che came to town with us on one of the many days that I needed to change a hundred-dollar bill into Cameroonian money. We took him to lunch at Friman's, where we had stopped on the day we went to Bafut. He seemed to think it might not be necessary for us to move out of our apartment the following week, and we wanted to believe him. Unfortunately, our hopes proved to be no more realistic than Che's dreams of a triumphant American music tour.

On another day we chose a different restaurant because of its name. It was called the Boston Restaurant, and was on the second floor of a building across from the entrance to the native market. A balcony hung above the street, which we reached by climbing a precarious, freestanding circular flight of metal steps that wrapped around a post that didn't seem very securely attached to the building.

Chicken and bushmeat were the only items on the menu that were available. We opted for chicken, and ordered pepper soup. I drank several beers to Lorna's one.

I had noticed a sign advertising pizza on a restaurant at the beginning of Commercial Street. It was opposite Friman's, and we met our English friend Phil there for beers one evening. It was a nice place to watch darkness fall on the main street. The restaurant was at the top of an enormous staircase, perhaps thirty stairs about twenty feet wide.

There was a level place at the top, onto which a few stores opened. There were a few tables there, as well as two tables at a landing, halfway down the flight of stairs. We took the tables at the top. It seemed an imposition to ask a waitress to run down ten steps whenever we needed more beer. Germaine worked for a moneylender that had an office above one of the stores on the other side of the street. We had arranged to meet her after work, along with her friend Mercy.

Earlier in the day, one could barely discern the cliffs of Upper Station looming beyond the buildings across the avenue, because of the thick morning haze. Now, with darkness falling, we could see the headlights of cars and share cabs as they made their way around the switchbacks on the mountain. Commercial Street below us was busy most of the day, but now, with people going home from work, share cabs were stopped all along the other side of the street, aggressively loading passengers. Almost all of the traffic at that time in the evening headed back toward the City Chemist's roundabout.

I remembered the pizza sign and asked the waitress if she could bring me a pizza, and she assured me that she could. Eventually, Mercy and Germaine showed up. Phil and I kept the beer coming. I checked on the progress of my pizza whenever our beers were replaced, and was always informed that it was in preparation. At last, nearly two hours later, our waitress brought the results to our table; a large round tray, tiled with some kind of crackers or biscuits, on which were heaped finely chopped tomatoes, an assemblage which had then been baked for an hour or so. She was so obviously proud of her performance that I told her it was one of the finest pizzas I had ever seen.

Two months earlier, we had been worried that we might run out of money, and be forced to leave Cameroon earlier than we had planned. Our stay in Bamenda had restored us to fiscal health and we could now consider buying some of the wonderful native crafts and artwork that we hadn't thought we could afford. There was a woodcarver's shop on Sonac Street that we had passed whenever we had gone to Upper Station, and we were interested in seeing what was sold there. It was a small building with only two rooms, on the hilly side of the street. The proprietor was a tall, slender gray-haired man in his 50s who, like his father and grandfather before him, had been a woodcarver all his life.

His shelves were jammed with his creations, as well as with a few things made by his ancestors, and his prices were excellent. The prices at the Prescraft Store had given us a good indication of what we should pay for things. Almost immediately, Lorna spotted a carved lion, with an insanely fierce expression, that was carved in the *lion passant* position, like the hallmark on British sterling silver. I loved it, but since Lorna had seen it first, I knew I would have to marry her to get it.

We bought a couple of masks, including a ceremonial mask on a stand from Bafut, and I bought a small string of black beads that women used around their waists to hold the grass that was used for skirts in less civilized times. Lorna found a large carving of a woman who was seated on a stool, suckling twins, which she bought as a present for Jeanne, whose twins were due soon after our return. We liked the woodcarver very much, and we talked about our respective families and histories for the rest of the day. There were many things in his shop that we wanted to see again, and he promised to also show us some treasures he kept in his home, on our next visit.

It was dinnertime when we left, and we took a share cab to Gracie's for our favorite dinner of thin steaks and fries. The restaurant was out of our favorite French bread, for which our cook apologized, but when our dinners came our favorite bread was there—he had found some for us!

It was beginning to get dark when we came back out onto Commercial Street. The market was closing, and throngs of share taxis had pulled to the curb on the opposite side of the street, to pack themselves with homegoers. We usually walked home from there. It was only about three blocks to the City Chemist's roundabout, and then a halfmile more to the left past all the establishments that had become so familiar to us on our daily sorties. On this evening, however, we were loaded down with our purchases, so we crossed the street to the taxis.

Taxis were vying for passengers, and three or four drivers at a time were trying to get us into their cabs. "Church Center?" we asked the drivers, and some seemed mystified, until finally one accepted, and stowed our bags in his trunk. But then, there was further controversy. Two large men who seemed to be running the whole show moved us to a different taxi, along with our luggage. "Center?" they kept asking, and we answered "Church Center".

Lorna sat in the back seat between two enormous women, and I sat in the front seat squeezed against the door by a woman so large that if a door had not been there, I could figuratively have been completely surrounded by her flesh. We didn't seem to share a common language with our driver.

When we came to the roundabout, we turned right along Sonac Street instead of left toward the Church Center. I wasn't alarmed, because a few days previously we had been taken on a small tour of the city, before being the last to be dropped off at the Church Center. When we reached the end of Sonac Street and started up the road to Upper Station I felt some exasperation, for we ought to have been home already. I was still relatively calm, however, because I thought we must surely be near the end of our trip, and would soon head back.

Lorna, however, was becoming very upset. The three enormous women all knew each other, and seemed to be aware of our predicament and enjoying it as well. Their laughter seldom stopped. We navigated the last of the switchbacks, and entered upon a long dark hilly road, where only an occasional vehicle passed us going in the opposite direction.

Lorna had passed the point of polite expostulation, and was demanding that our driver stop the cab immediately and let us out, or she would jump screaming from the moving vehicle. Something in her behavior eventually penetrated the language barrier, and the driver pulled over to the side of the road and stopped. We emerged from the vehicle on an especially dark downgrade. There were few houses and many trees, but somehow a small crowd assembled. We got our bags from the trunk, but now the driver wanted to be paid. We naturally refused to give him anything, and a discussion arose among the onlookers about the validity or lack of validity of his claim. Our side prevailed, and he finally left for what we found out was the town of Santa, still several miles away, which the dispatchers across from Gracie's thought we were saying when we said 'Center'.

Several of the people in the small crowd were very kind to us. There was a small nightclub in the trees off the road and we met a man who was leaving for home from there. He told us that he lived a couple of miles in our direction. He stayed with us until we could flag down a taxi returning to Bamenda. When we finally found a taxi with sufficient empty seats, he talked to the driver to make sure we weren't charged too much, since fares after dark are negotiable. He rode with us as far as the place he lived and stopped the cab. When he was let out on the road, he stood in the headlights of the taxi to write down his name and address for us, in case the opportunity arose to pursue a friendship at a later date. The cost of our return trip was 200 CFAs (80 cents). That was only double the usual price for trips around Bamenda, no matter how short.

CH 17

We meet Robert Graham

This Flower
has the
colors of
the Cameroon
Flag.

On Sunday, we had to pack all of our things for our move to different quarters. It was amazing that the contents of two backpacks could morph into so much stuff, especially considering the fact that we had left so many of our things with Elsa in Buea. I emptied my dresser and Lorna emptied her wardrobe, and we spread the contents over our beds and every other free surface in our room. There were the food and supplies that we used daily, but in addition we had added a small library of Cameroonian literature to the writing and art materials we had brought from home. Lorna had bought several paperback novels by Cameroonian novelists from the street sellers along Commercial Street. I was used to the low prices that paperbacks fetch at yard sales and secondhand stores in our country, and I was critical of her paying too much for badly dog-eared copies of Cameroonian novels from a bookseller who occupied a few hundred square feet of pavement in front of a bank on Commercial Street.

He set his books out flat in rows, and brought them daily to his location. Many of them were ancient, well-used instructional books that would be discarded in the United States, but here they were offered for the equivalent of a few dollars apiece. Lorna had overridden my objections and paid what she had to for what became a wonderful though shabby collection of Cameroonian novelists like Mongo Beti, Ferdinand Oyono, and Kenjo Jumban. She had also made a friend of the book dealer, who forever after greeted us effusively.

We had gone back to our woodcarver and bought more carvings, which were proving to cause a difficult exercise in packing geometry. He had sold us a couple of large, zip up tapestry bags to ship our purchases home in. We used our clothing and collectible textiles we had purchased to protect our carvings from damage.

We were just beginning to make some headway with our packing when there was a knock on our front door. I opened it to find a large and rather plump young man standing there. He introduced himself as our nephew, and I immediately knew from the family chart that Clara had given us that this was Robert Graham Luke, who had been driving his mother on the day we met him coming back from Wum.

We cleared a chair for him, but after the hugs and introduction, he continued to circulate around the room, picking up and examining everything lying about. Lorna, remembering the troubles with Noah, did not want him to touch our cell phone, but Robert picked it up and began experimenting with it. Lorna took it back from him, but then he wanted to see my camera. I showed it to him without allowing him to handle it, but next he noticed the Timex watch I was wearing. He wanted me to take it off so that he could examine it better. He liked it, and asked if we would send him one when we returned to the U.S.

Robert only stayed for twenty minutes or so, since he had a friend with a small baby waiting in his car. After he left, we finished our packing, and the next morning Che helped us move to our new room, in a different guesthouse, across the street and further up the hill.

It was a long building like the other guesthouses, but rather than a single line of rooms opening onto a long porch facing the street, our new building had a porch along the back as well, with another line of rooms, one of which we were given. We didn't have our own bathroom, but shared instead a communal bathroom a few doors down from us. We looked out onto a wide grassy area, above and behind the Administration Building, with a small church at the high end that had a New England feel, despite the tropical setting.

We now lacked cooking facilities, and consequently took most of our meals downtown, although a few times we took advantage of dinners prepared for the conference. They were usually very good: a large chunk of beef, cooked like a pot roast with gravy, and boiled yams, or a very good chicken stew. We always showed up at the appointed meal times, and we were through with our meals and leaving before the conferees began straggling in. They ended their day with a religious service that usually ran well into dinnertime, and in the morning they liked to sleep late.

A secular group like the Language Association was usually early for breakfast, and occasionally travelers like our English friend Philip would share our table in the morning. We enjoyed our breakfasts more when conferences were being held, because the table would be piled high with fresh batards of French bread, instead of the dense Cameroonian equivalent of Wonder Bread that was our usual fare. It meant that someone had to make a special trip to the boulangerie on Sonac Street, which was the nearest place that sold it.

Reverend Joseph met us as we were leaving breakfast one morning to tell us that the Moderator was coming for a visit of a few days at the Church Center, in order to dedicate a new church in Bafut on the following Sunday. He hoped we would attend. The head of the church was Fung's brother-in-law, and held the position Fung's father once held. His wife, who was Fung's sister Cynthia, was coming to Bamenda with him, and they were expected to stay with Reverend Joseph and Jeanne at their residence.

We had met him only once before, when we had visited his home with Paul and Elsa on our arrival in Cameroon, although we had seen Cynthia more often. She had invited us to breakfast once, and we saw her again at Elsa's party. It was only after we came to Bamenda that we gained some inkling of the prestige with which he was regarded by the faithful. I saw his picture on the cover of a magazine downtown. It was a formal portrait of pastor, standing with his hands clasped, and wearing the crimson stole of his rank. The magazine identified him as the leader of the Protestant church. I saw the photograph displayed in many of the homes I visited, in the same fashion that devout Catholics display pictures of the Pope. I later learned that Pastor had recently been elected to a five-year term as the Chairman of the African Council of Churches, a position formerly held by Bishop Desmond Tutu of South Africa. The position required frequent travel, and he was due to fly soon to Nairobi to chair an international conference for reconciliation on the tenth anniversary of the Rwandan massacre.

We had been planning to leave Bamenda to visit Foumban and we would already have done so, had we not been waiting for Claudia to come from America with Lorna's replacement pills. Now that Pastor and Cynthia were coming, we hoped we could persuade them to carry all our purchases back to Buea, so that we wouldn't risk breaking them on our further travels.

We went back to visit our woodcarver friend, and made several more purchases from his home. His workshop was on a hill about fifteen feet high that edged Sonac Street. The land behind it dropped sharply into a ravine about eighty feet deep before rising again for a couple of hundred feet with hillside residences that looked down on the street.

Our woodcarver lived in a house at the bottom of the ravine, and the path down was extremely steep. His house, like many of the houses in Bamenda, resembled the ranch houses we build in the U.S. Lorna and I sat on a comfortable sofa while he showed us carvings that his father had made, and a few things that he had collected. We bought several masks and I bought a wonderful piece of King's cloth, about five feet wide and nine feet long. I had seen a slightly larger piece for sale at the Prescraft Store on Commercial Street that was much more expensive. Fung had talked about King's cloth before we came to Cameroon, and I had seen pictures of it. In our Cameroonian guidebook kings or fons were shown with a backdrop of King's cloth as a wallhanging behind them.

It was an attractive, indigo-dyed cotton fabric that was covered with lines of traditional symbols. We tend to consider cloth made of cotton as something cheap, but King's cloth is rare and expensive. The thread that it's made from is handspun, and then loomed into narrow strips twelve or fourteen inches wide on portable handlooms. The strips are sewed together to form the desired width, and the resulting bolt of cloth is sent to a different area where dyeing is done. The designs and symbols are first drawn on the cloth, and raffia is sewn over them so that when the cloth is immersed in indigo dye, the designs are left natural. The raffia is then removed to complete the project. We carefully packed all our carvings in the large zip-up bags we bought from our woodcarver, padding everything with King's cloth or extra clothing. Germaine's family and Menad continued to visit us in our new location, and our week in exile passed quickly.

Sunday was the day of the new church dedication and Reverend Joseph arranged a ride to Bafut for us with Reverend Nkweti. He was the senior minister of the Bamenda region, and the curate of a parish in Upper Station. He was a tall and courtly gray haired man and he drove a Toyota sedan. The road to Bafut was now familiar to us, an easy ride of about fifteen miles, and with our driver's clerical collar, we passed through checkpoints without stopping. We talked about our families. Lorna told everyone she met about Jeanne's twins that were due, which was always an instant passport to prestige. Rev, Nkweti responded with some pride that he was a grandfather of twins.

A large crowd had gathered for the dedication ceremony of the new parish. There were many who were clergy, and some who had driven long distances to be there. The minister of the new parish was a very pleasant and gregarious woman, the only woman I had ever met in Cameroon who had an ecclesiastical function. She had laid out a large buffet breakfast for the visiting dignitaries, among whom we were included, and she seemed very much at ease among scores of men in clerical collars. Pastor had arrived before us, and he spoke with us while we were eating. We met a group of Swiss that represented the European branch of the Protestant Church, but the growth of the denomination in Cameroon had been so great that the Cameroonian Church was now the dominant branch.

The new church was large enough to hold several hundred people, and it was filled to capacity for the occasion. It was nearly complete, except for a roof. Lorna and I took seats among the clergy, in two rows behind the lectern, facing the church full of congregants. We were next to a large table set at an angle in the front corner, at which sat the Fon of Bafut, resplendent in a gold-trimmed light blue fabric, and his queen, who had been our guide when we visited the palace with Che.

Most of the morning was taken up by a service, which was followed by the formal dedication of the new parish. The head of the church performed the official ceremony. A fund-raising period then began, with a few words from the Fon, and his pledge of half a million CFAs, more than a thousand dollars toward the construction of the roof. For the next hour, people stood and made pledges, and a running total was announced, until the estimated cost of the roof had been met (approximately twenty thousand dollars).

We didn't get back to the Church Center in Bamenda until late afternoon. Reverend Nkweti let us off at the Administration Building, where several ministers had gathered to say goodbye to the Moderator, who was returning to Buea the next day. We were introduced to Dr. Su, an older prelate who had known Fung's father. Dr. Su was a tall, distinguished man whom we only met in passing, but he expressed a desire to meet with us in the near future. Reverend Joseph was in the group with him, and set up a meeting for us a few days later.

Dr. Su lived in Bafut, and Reverend Joseph drove us to his house. His house was unlike any other that I saw in Cameroon. It was a large, comfortable arts and crafts bungalow. It was cool and spacious. Every Cameroonian home that I had previously seen was furnished with massive, overstuffed furniture, produced in all the local shops with rich upholstery fabrics and ponderous wooden facings. Dr. Su's house was furnished with tastefully arranged Danish modern furniture; his deceased wife had been Swiss. Reverend Joseph left Lorna and me to talk with the doctor and he promised to come back in two hours. I was surprised to learn that Dr. Su was in his late eighties; he seemed like a much younger man.

He had written extensively about Africa's problems, and we discussed many of them. We bought his most recent book, on national education policies in sub-Saharan Africa, which dealt especially with the Cameroonian experience. It was different from the others in that three different European languages, French, German, and English, were grafted onto an indigenous culture in which more than two hundred native languages were spoken.

We talked about the important contribution of the local cultures to national identity, and how it should be expressed, and balanced with the needs of a national system. We were fascinated by the Dr.'s exposition of the history of the missions to the Bafut region, and we were surprised to find we had been talking for more than two hours when Reverend Joseph came to take us back to Bamenda.

When our week of 'exile' ended, we moved back into our apartment. It was on a Monday morning, the day after the church dedication. While Pastor and Cynthia had been staying with Reverend Joseph and Jeanne at the director's house, Pastor had taken the opportunity to make a series of formal visits to parishes around Bamenda. Now, as he was returing to Buea, Lorna and I wanted to take advantage of it. We packed our recent purchases in a large carpetbag, and brought them to the director's house and gave them to John, the Moderator's driver.

We hadn't been happy with the prospect of dragging that bag with its precious cargo on our further trips by bus to Bali and Foumban, not to mention the daylong trip back to Buea. Almost every time we had planned to leave Bamenda, we had postponed it, but now we were down to our final days there. Claudia had arrived from the United States, and would pass through Bamenda on her way to visit her father's grave in Wum in one more week. She had with her the Commit pills that Clara had sent for Lorna's nicotine withdrawal symptoms. We would leave after that.

CH 18

Bali, Foumban, farewell Bamenda

The rainy season was approaching. Our friend Philip had moved on, and Richard and Sandra, an American couple from Colorado, arrived at the Center on our first afternoon back at our apartment. They were a trim couple in their forties, who had been helping to build a chimpanzee sanctuary near Cameroon's border with the Central African Republic. It was close to an area that we had passed through on the train. They had taken a vacation to make a tour around the country, and had just arrived from Wum.

Richard was wearing broken glasses. He had a patch on one eye, and a bandage on his forehead. The taxi in which they had been riding from Wum had been engaged in an accident, and he had been patched up by a local doctor. The taxi, an old Toyota Corolla, had been loaded with nine people, which had forced the driver to hang out the window while he tried to operate it. This, however, had not slowed him down. He came around a blind curve at high speed, and smashed into a truck blocking the road. Richard had been in the front and had hit the windshield, while Sandra, in the back, had been padded by the other passengers. They told me that the taxi had been a total loss, but that only the driver was seriously injured. They needed some groceries, so I walked with Sandra to the nearest store, and picked up a few things for myself as well.

Germaine and her mother visited frequently, often accompanied by her sister Cynthia, if she was home from the university in Dschang. They often brought dinner that they had cooked, and we sat around with candles to keep the insects at bay. Germaine had taken her degree in African studies, and told us her experiences in collecting regional folk tales in distant villages.

Before we left Bamenda, we wanted to take all our friends out for a farewell dinner. It would take place the following Sunday, which was a week away. We planned to gather at our apartment, and hire a taxi to take us to a suitable restaurant. Meanwhile, Robert Graham Luke visited us a second time. We told him about our travel plans, including Bali and Foumban, and Robert suggested that he could drive us to those locations, and even back to Buea when we were ready to return. Compared with the rigors of our other travel options, it was llike being offered a magic carpet. We invited Robert to our farewell dinner, and he offered to drive everyone.

Six of our friends came to our apartment on Sunday morning. Besides Robert, there were Che and Patience, Germaine, Cynthia, and their mother. We drove first to our favorite restaurant on Upper Station, with its beautiful view of the city, but were disappointed to find that it was closed. Someone recommended we should try 'Dreamland', a very nice restaurant on Commercial Street, and we drove there next. It occupied the second floor of a building on the next block from where I had found the 'pizza'. There, eight of us found a large, round table on a balcony overlooking the street. We ordered our drinks, but were driven indoors by the smells emanating from a sewer-cleaning operation, which surprisingly was being carried out on a Sunday.

We took our beer to an inside table that was more elegant, with white tablecloths and soft lights, and we made our choices from the menu. When our meals were served, Robert Graham was very severe with our waitress, and sent his plate back to the kitchen three times before it met with his satisfaction. When our bill came, Robert picked it up and questioned the waitress at length about every item listed, until he felt satisfied and passed it to me for payment.

After dinner, some of our party left, and Robert drove the rest of us to a Billiard Hall in a part of Bamenda that Lorna and I were unfamiliar with. It was behind the huge native market that we often shopped at, and next to an open dump of several acres, many of which were burning. We watched as Robert played several games, and won many of them. He seemed to be on friendly terms with most of the other patrons. It was getting dark as we left.

The next day Robert came by around 11:00 A.M. to take us to Bali. He drove to a filling station where we filled his car with gas before we set out. Robert lavished care on his Corolla; it had been brown when we had first seen it, at the time we met his mother on the road from Wum, but he had since had it painted blue, and he had decorated the hood with a stick-on Mercedes finial, of which he was immensely proud.

Bali was an important Fondom, located about twelve miles southwest of Bamenda. The drive there took us through some of the prettiest country that I had seen anywhere in Cameroon. It was a landscape that would rival the most attractive areas of Vermont, with open hills and impressive stands of eucalyptus trees, tall and straight and topping a hundred feet. Road cuts exposed deep red earth rather than upthrust rock. We were stopped by a police checkpoint. The officer in charge, a Lieutenant, was a friend of Robert's, and he joined us for the ride into town. We stopped at a general store near the center of town, where we bought cold drinks and a telephone card for Robert, who wanted to telephone his mother in Douala.

Next we stopped by another of Robert's friends, who had a farm on a nearby country road, and then drove to the palace of theFon. We paid our fee to a guide who served us an aperitif of palm wine, and then guided us through the palace. The palace had a large number of rooms and a beautiful location, but lacked decorative elements, giving it a stark ambience.

After leaving the palace, we visited with another of Robert's friends, the local postmaster. He was a courteous man, who served us Coca-Cola as we sat in his living room. On the way back to Bamenda, the car developed an exhaust problem. Robert got a repair estimate from a mechanic's shop on the outskirts of town, and surprisingly we needed more gasoline at this point. Of course we paid, and we gave Robert the money needed to fix his exhaust as well. He was becoming expensive.

We had committed ourselves to using Robert for our transportation needs, and we planned to make a trip to Foumban before returning to Buea at the end of the week. Germaine had done some of her degree work in Foumban, and wanted to visit it again. She decided to take the day off from work and come with us when we went there, which turned out to be Wednesday, since Robert needed all of Tuesday to remedy his car problems.

Robert came early on Wednesday, and Germaine had arrived early as well, and we set out in high spirits for what we expected to be a long trip. In order to reach Foumban, a hundred and fifty kilometers away, it would be necessary to drive first to Bafoussam, the halfway point, before heading east into West Province. On the way we passed through Santa, the town we nearly ended up in the night we were 'kidnapped'.

As soon as we left Bamenda, Robert began to speed. Lorna was sitting in the backseat with Germaine, and kept asking him to slow down, but it only incited him to go faster. Soon after we got on the road to Santa, we passed a native market with people all over the road. Robert began blowing his horn as soon as they were in sight, and kept it blaring all the way through the congested area, which he took at high speed. No one was killed, but that set the tone for the trip.

The large city of Bafoussam barely slowed him down, although we made a stop at a boulangerie for picnic ingredients. Bafoussam is French speaking, and seemed to have much more economic activity than Bamenda, indicating, I thought, a definite bias toward Francophone regions by the national government.

I later discussed this theory with a friend of Fung's, who ascribed differences to the industriousness of the Bameleke people. The trip to Foumban was nearly three hours. After our long sojourn in temperate Bamenda, it felt like we were back in the far north. The day was hot and dry, and the few trees were palms. We were glad that we hadn't moved there, since the inn Dabala had found for us was nearly ten miles from the active part of town.

The culture of Foumban was distinctly different from the culture of the grassland kingdom where we had been living. It was the seat of a hereditary sultanate that dated back to 1394. In the early twentieth century, it had had a remarkably capable ruler by the name of Ibraham Njoya, who was the sixteenth sultan of his line. He built an imposing palace and museum, which was architecturally based on the German Governor's palace in Buea. The palace was at the end of an impressive drive, along which memorials to former leaders and battles had been erected. It opened before the palace onto a broad, circular drive, dominated by a fierce looking equestrian statue of a rearing horse with a triumphant ruler with raised scimitar.

The first two floors of the palace served as a museum, where glass cases displayed sumptuous gowns and other items of personal use from former dynasties: musical instruments, jewelry, and tools for torture and warfare. I remember a particularly grisly war club, with a bulbous end, that had been enhanced with the lower jawbones of slain opponents.

Several display cases were devoted to samples of the Bamaun script that Sultan Ibraham Njoya had created around 1896 to resist colonial homogenization. It was an interesting alphabet that consisted of seventy signs or Shumum, as they are called: sixty-five are consonants, and five are vowels. The Sultan created forty schools that taught only Shumum in his domain, and the language was loved, and flourished until 1924, when French colonial authorities abolished it and closed down the schools.

After leaving the palace, we drove to the *Village des Artisans*, a large congregation of workshops that were famous throughout the country for the quality of their work. The Lebanese owner of the restaurant in N'Gaoundere had told us he owned a shop here. Lorna and Germaine went off shopping for nearly two hours while I chatted in French with a nearby group of workmen. Robert paced in frantic exasperation and boredom.

When the women finally reappeared, Lorna was triumphantly holding a large wonderfully carved wooden bowl that she bought for very little money because it had a broken handle on one side. It had begun at a high price, but the maker finally almost gave it to her, and she felt it would make an elegant prsentation for soup or salads.

Robert hustled us all back on the road, but this time, Lorna was able to slow him down from reckless to merely fast by mimicking the sound of his horn blowing whenever he began to blow it. Just outside Foumban, we stopped at a native market for some fruit and drinks, and I photographed some very attractive women who were selling there. Beyond the market, there was a long, straight stretch of road, somewhere along which the Mercedes hood ornament blew off the car. Robert was very unhappy, and we retraced the last mile several times with all of us checking the edge of the road, before he gave up.

We came upon a roadside hut, made of bent bows and long grasses, and we made a picnic there for a late lunch. I took pictures of all of us in the hut, including a friendly truck driver who visited with us there. We always remember where we lose choice little things that we are fond of, and it was here that I last saw our really neat stainless steel Swiss army knife, which we used for everything.

Robert was rather subdued, and drove sensibly for the rest of the trip. As we approached Bamenda, we saw evidence of a violent rainsquall on the wet road, with many broken branches strewn about. While passing through Upper Station, we decided to stop at the doorcarver's shop because Germaine wanted to talk with them and find out their names. As we pulled into the parking area of the restaurant across the road, Robert drove into a hole at the edge of the pavement, and broke a shock absorber. The entire car listed so badly that we were unable to continue, and had to take a share taxi home while Robert's car limped to a repair shop.

Claudia and Elsa arrived that evening, and we were surprised that Nia was with them. He drove the car they had rented. It was good to see him again, and we realized how much we had missed him after being together so long in the north. Their rented car had given them trouble, and they were somewhat exasperated with it. They would need to pay to have it repaired, and collect from the rental agency later.

We also needed to have a car repaired, which included a new Mercedes hood ornament; Robert had become very expensive, although the hood ornament was plastic and only 1,000 CFAs (two dollars). It seemed we were hemorrhaging money again, and we were undecided whether to continue with Robert for our return to Buea, or cut our losses, say goodbye to Robert, and return to Buea the way we had come. We finally sat down with him, and laid out the exact amount of money we would give him as our share of the trip. We planned to leave in two more days.

Early on the day of our departure, there was a knock on our front door. It was Menad, and he had a present for me. He had noticed that I carried my eyeglasses loose, and he bought a slipcase for them with money he saved from posing. He was looking forward to receiving his final marks for the year later that day, and I wished him luck. He was a top student in his class, and he expected to do well.

We didn't leave until the next day, however, and we saw Menad one more time, a very unhappy Menad. The school had not released his grades, because he owed fees that were not paid, and he didn't have the money to do so. He didn't ask for our help, but we most certainly would have tried to help him, if we had had any money available. Elsa had the balance of our funds back in Buea, and we didn't know how much we would need before we left the country.

Coming to Bamenda by bus had taken a whole day, but driving back with Robert took about five hours, and we found the trip pleasant. We stopped again at the boulangerie in Bafoussam, and bought sliced sandwich meats and cheeses and made enough sandwiches for the trip.

This time, Robert drove at reasonable speeds, and we passed through some very beautiful areas. The deep, wooded defiles of the north gave way to a region of solitary great hills, through which we wound for the next few hours. At one point, we got behind an oil truck, spraying oil from the caps of its tanks, and it made such a mess of the windshield that it was impossible to see well enough to drive. Robert pulled into a service station and had the windshield cleaned. When the clerk had finished the job, Robert inspected it carefully and found several spots that he had missed along the edge, and brought him back to finish the job.

For the most part, Robert was a pleasant young man, but Lorna and I were left shaking our heads in wonder at his arrogance toward those who served him. He had one particular habit that annoyed Lorna enormously. Whenever we stopped at a toll station, rather than ask for money, he would simply put his hand out to her, palm up, and say nothing.

The road from Bamenda to Buea ran first through Douala, where Robert lived, and he wanted to stop and see his mother, who lived just off the main road in Bonaberi, the part of Douala that lies beyond the Wouri River. She was caring for her mother, who was bedridden, and I took several pictures of the entire family. We stayed for about an hour, and then drove out to Buea, arriving back at the Protestant Guesthouse before dark.

CH 19

Farewell Buea and Cameroon

Hotel du RAIL
N'Gaoundere, Cameroon
there were No Bird –
only one small one
... *Sized cockroacher*
in Bath. Maybe Three
... *became important* ...

With so many members of Fung's family living in the vicinity, returning to Buea was like coming home. We were welcomed back like old friends by the manager of the guesthouse, and also by the two women who worked with him, and we even got our old room back. We had especially liked because it got the morning sun. The haze of the harmattan had passed with the season, and on most days, we were able to see the coast of Limbe and the sea beyond from the front of the guesthouse. At night, the lights of Douala, nearly thirty miles away, were visible. We went to the treasurer's office and reclaimed the balance of our funds, and were pleased to find nearly a third of the money we had budgeted for our trip was still there.

We wanted to be sure of getting back to the U.S. before Jeanne's twins were born, so we decided to move our flights up a few weeks, which would save us the trouble of renewing our visas. Of course the airline imposed a financial penalty for this change, but we paid it readily. Two weeks remained of our stay in Cameroon.

On the first day back in Buea, we went to a trade show in Limbe that Elsa had wanted to see. The show took place in a dusty soccer stadium, in which the vendors had set up rows of booths in open-sided tents. Their displays consisted mainly of modern jewelry and personal hygiene products. Elsa and Lorna enjoyed trying on the jewelry, and Elsa found a necklace she liked. She had done so much for us that it was a pleasure to be able to buy it for her as a gift.

It was time for lunch when we left the trade show. We took a taxi to the nearby botanical gardens, which had a small restaurant at the rear. It occupied an idyllic location beside the ocean, where we sat in a breezy gazebo and dined on steak, beer, and French fries. During lunch, we looked out on a small bay filled with tiny islands. After lunch, we explored the gardens, reading the labels on plants and trees. At the end of the day, we caught one of the small buses that are used for local travel in Cameroon, which took us to the motor park at Mile 17, where we found another bus to return to Buea.

Lorna and I traveled frequently to Douala for shopping and lunch, and we always stopped at Zepol's for some little treat. Douala, with a population of one and a third million people, is more than twice the size of Boston. The scale of buildings in the downtown area reminded me of Boston's Washington Street. We had lunch one day at an Armenian restaurant six blocks beyond Zepol's. At the corner of a major intersection, we passed a completely naked woman, who was sitting on the sidewalk with her back against a light pole. One of her legs looked like it had been burned from the knee down. Its skin was all bubbly, as if it had been immersed in scalding liquid. Like the naked man in Maroua, no one paid any attention, and I remember Maggie's statement: "What does one do with such people?"

There are large sections of Douala with ruined streets, as we had discovered on the day we took the bus to Yaounde. That day, we had passed through parts of the city clogged with teeming masses of people jammed into shanties or shopping in the massive native market. However, other parts of the city were prosperous neighborhoods of quiet, leafy streets with well-kept apartments and red-tiled roofs. It was in such an area that we found the *Marche des Fleurs*. It was a bazaar of traditional native crafts that occupied the interior of a block where small shops displayed stylish women's clothing.

There were stalls selling every kind of decorative object, many of which we had seen for sale at Prescraft in Bamenda. We had desired them then, but didn't buy at that time because of the uncertainty of our finances. Most of the stalls specialized in particular items, like masks, beads, or musical instruments. I bought a chess set like the one I had desired ever since I had first seen one in the Prescraft store. I was able to choose from scores of cast bronze sets that the stall had to offer. Each pawn of my set was a warrior brandishing a weapon: a large, curved sword for the pale brass warriors, and massive clubs for those in blackened bronze.

As we made our way through the market, it soon became evident that an informal telegraph system was broadcasting our progress. Lorna bought several strands of heavy, bronze beads, and passed up those whose owners wouldn't meet our price. When we left the market, we sat for a few minutes in the parking lot, to inventory our purchases. One of the vendors we had passed up found us there, and accepted a previous offer we had made.

On one of our last trips to Douala, we were finally able to get a view of Mount Cameroon in its full glory. We were waiting for a bus at the Mile 17 motor park. Without the haze of the harmattan, the mountain rose clearly from the 3,000foot platform on which we were standing. For the first time, we had an inkling of its true majesty and power.

Several climbing groups stayed at our guesthouse where they met mountain guides who assembled porters for the climb. It usually took three days. We met a young Belgian student who had been working for an NGO (Non Governmental Organization) for a year, and whose parents had come to visit with him and climb the mountain. They began their climb in high spirits, but returned after only two days because of dense mists that reduced visibility nearly to zero. They felt that it was pointless to go on if they couldn't see anything.

A few days later, a large American group arrived. They asked me where they could buy sandwich ingredients for their trip, and I took two of them in a share taxi to Beno's Boulangerie. We had to walk the last quarter mile, however, when our driver informed us that he didn't have any brakes and couldn't venture onto the steep incline where the shop was located.

One night during our last days in Buea, a violent storm arose some time after midnight, with winds so strong we feared the entire guesthouse could blow off the mountain. It was of short duration, however, and was followed by a day of exceptional beauty.

On Easter Sunday, I attended a three-hour service at the Protestant Church. Lorna missed it because she was involved with a group of drawings she was working on. Three distinct choral groups took part in the Easter service, all of which were so outstanding that I wanted to find out if it was possible to buy CDs of their music. Elsa told me that they were planning to produce some.

The nearer we came to the end of our stay in Cameroon, the dearer Fung's family became for us. Fung's sister Claudia, whom we had first met at Clara and Fung's wedding, was on her first visit back to her homeland since she had emigrated. After she had visited her father's grave in Wum, she returned to Buea to stay with her sister Cynthia and Pastor at the Moderator's official residence in the same room that she had grown up in, her father having been the previous Moderator.

Claudia was scheduled to return to the U.S. on the same flight as Lorna and I. A few days before our departure, pastor scheduled a dinner party to celebrate Claudia's and our visit. Nearly forty people attended, including most of the dignitaries of the Church hierarchy. His large living room comfortably acommodated everyone. An elaborate buffet was laid out in their dining room that was constantly replenished by the young women who worked in the house.

Pastor enjoyed good wine. He enjoyed drinking it, talking about it, and sharing it. Whenever I visited him, he would choose a bottle of some vintage for my perusal and opinion, not for me to sample, but to drink the entire bottle. That way, he needn't concern himself with 'topping up' each person's glass. Lorna showed the pictures of Clara and Fung's wedding to the assembled guests, and presented the family members with large pictures of the couple that she had used to make their wedding announcements.

On our last night in Cameroon, we invited Elsa and Paul for beer and snacks at the guesthouse. We had been to Douala that day, and we had bought some cheese from Zepol's, which we served on batards from our local boulangerie. We talked about the differences and the common elements of our two countries. Elsa had been to the United States, but Paul had never been out of Cameroon. A U.S. supermarket is difficult to explain to someone who has never seen one. One obvious difference, of course, was the great imbalance of wealth between the two countries, but it was interesting how this played out in every day life.

Life in Cameroon is like life as it existed in our country prior to World War II. Everything at that time was expensive, and therefore valued. Schoolteachers passed out paper one sheet at a time, and students were required to use both sides. Clothing was mended rather than thrown away, and food stores were tiny. In recent years, we have become a consumer-driven society, with a throwaway culture. The processed food delivered by our vaunted supermarkets has not been helpful for the health of our country. Cameroon, on the other hand, is a wonderful food producer where the fruit of the land is available everywhere, natural, unpackaged, and cheap.

At the end of the evening, Elsa and Paul raised, as delicately as they could, their wish that Lorna and I could somehow be instrumental in helping their sons, Luke and Matthew, gain admission to the United States. They were bright and handsome young men of college age, with an older sister who worked as a lawyer in Belgium. Our response had to be equivocal. There was little we could do, with U.S. immigration policy being what it is, but we agreed to take a series of photographs showing us in various associations with the young men. The photographs would serve as proof of our real connection with them in any application they might make for American visas.

Our flight to Zurich was scheduled for 9:20 P.M. next day. That afternoon, a caravan of three cars gathered at the Moderator's house as we took some final photographs. Fung's aunt from Douala wanted to ride with us to the airport. Cynthia and Elsa came along, as well as Claudia, who was on our flight. Elsa's husband, Paul, rode with us for part of the trip, but had to leave for a business appointment near the outskirts of Buea.

When we entered Cameroon, we brought large suitcases with us, to hold all the presents that the American branch of the family was sending to the Cameroonian branch. Now the large suitcases were going in the opposite direction, filled with presents for the American branch. For example, certain spices that are not available in the U.S., much African clothing, and even the familiar "33" or Castel beers, which were received with such delight that it was worth the luggage space to carry some. Claudia was bringing five enormous suitcases, each of which appeared to greatly exceed the weight limits. Fung's aunt gave Lorna and me a set of wooden salad bowls as a farewell gift.

Our caravan arrived at the airport in late afternoon. The luggage check in was not easy. All of Claudia's bags were rejected; not one of them was even close to the requirements. It was then that the director of security for the airport was called, and everything went better after that, because he was a family member. Changes were made, items were switched around, and there were many re-weighings, but in the end everything was somehow accepted. The workers who checked us in showed us enormous respect and consideration, and our porter did not even want to accept our tips. He did so only upon our insistence. It was dark when our flight took off, and we were finally heading back to our ordinary lives, which now seemed to be something that had taken place in a dream. The marabout had predicted that we would come back to Cameroon, and we hope that all his predictions will prove to be correct.

POSTSCRIPT

Some unfinished business

Menad

Soon after we got home, Reverend Joseph and his wife Jeanne came to the U.S. to attend the graduation of their daughter from a law school in Maryland. A second daughter lived in Minnesota. Like so many Cameroonian families who could afford to do so, they had sent their children to either Europe or the United States for better opportunities in life. Reverend Joseph had previously visited the United States, briefly, for an ecclesiastical conference that had been held at MIT. His wife had never been out of Cameroon.

I telephoned them at their daughter's home im Maryland, and asked if they could fit a trip to Boston into their itinerary. Reverend Joseph liked the idea, but confessed that their travel budget wouldn't allow for it. They had been very gracious to us in Bamenda, and Lorna and I wanted to repay them for their kindness. We invited them to stay as guests at my house in Arlington, and we offered to send airline tickets if that might enable them to come. They accepted our invitation, and a few days later, Lorna and I drove to Manchester, N.H. to meet their Southwest Airlines flight from Maryland.

Lorna and I had been living independently, in our respective houses, for the few weeks between our return from Cameroon and the beginning of our summer rental in Truro. We were due to move to the cape that very week. Reverend Joseph and Jeanne were able to spend a week with us. During the first few days of their visit, we took them around the Greater Boston area, and especially to Cambridge and MIT, which Reverend Joseph had wanted to see again. Then there was family to meet: Clara and Fung in Chelsea, Fung's large family in North of Boston, and Jeanne and her husband in Truro.

With the birth of her twins now imminent, Jeanne was staying at a hospital on the Cape. We visited her when we drove our guests to Truro to stay overnight at the house we had rented. We took Reverend Joseph and Jeanne for dinner in Provincetown and joined the throngs in streets where African costume did not seem out of place. Reverend Joseph's reaction to Ben and Jerry's ice cream was amusing. It was the first time he had ever tried it, and from the expression on his face, one might think that his mouth was on fire. I suspect that he enjoyed it less than I had enjoyed the grasshoppers in Cameroon.

A large branch of Fung's family, including his mother, lived in North of Boston. Reverend Joseph was related to them in some way, and also served as the administrator for Fung's father's estate. There were some matters that he wanted to discuss with Fung's mother, and so, at the end of their visit, Clara and Fung drove them to North of Boston, where Fung's family took care of getting them back to Manchester for their return flight to Maryland.

Before they left, they were able to help Lorna and me with some business that we had left unfinished in Bamenda. We were greatly distressed that we had not been able to help our young friend Menad. The balance of our funds had then been at the church office in Buea, and we were unsure what our future requirements could entail. However, we returned from Cameroon with nearly five hundred dollars in Cameroonian currency, which we now gave to Reverend Joseph along with an explanation of Menad's predicament with school fees. We tried to tell him as well as we were able what Menad had told us about where his house was located. We later heard that it took several months for Reverend Joseph and Jeanne to find him, but they were finally able to pass along our help to him. Several months later, we received a letter from Menad's mother, thanking Lorna and me for being the Lord's instruments. We wanted to contact Menad again, but the e-mail address he had given me never worked.

We moved to Truro for the summer, and Jeanne gave birth to the twins Ella and Anders about a week later, near the end of May. For half the summer they were our nextdoor neighbors, and for the weeks when their house was rented we all lived together. It was an interesting place to stay. A number of detached single-rental units were associated with the house we rented and several artists lived there for the summer. With the inclusion of Jeanne and Conrad, who are both artists, we formed a flourishing art colony.

My writing went on at a desultory pace. I walked the beach daily for long distances, with the dunes on the one side and the sea on the other. Cameroon shared a distant shore of the sea, and here I felt connected to those I had met there. Provincetown, with its restaurants and galleries, was only minutes away. There it seemed that Cameroon was something I had once dreamed.

It was nearly October when the season ended, and Lorna and I had to decide whether or not we were going to resume living separately in our own homes. We wanted to be together all the time, but Lorna found living in my house difficult, and consequently I found myself living most of the time in her small Chelsea apartment.

I missed my belongings, most of all my books, but Lorna wanted to do art, and my house didn't have enough space for it without some major dislocations. We wanted to find a house that would accommodate both our needs. We spent a lot of time looking at houses in Cambridge and Somerville, but couldn't find a house in either place that we both liked and could afford.

With summer over, we were in the third week of this new, unsatisfactory routine. We were lying, reading on Lorna's bed one

Sunday morning. It was the only place in her house where one could read, watch television, or otherwise relax. We had just finished the Sunday paper, and we were glancing through a few magazines that were lying around. Boston magazine had a page of houses advertised that were taken from a wide area, and a house in New Bedford caught my eye. It was about an hour from Boston.

New Bedford had been at one time the richest city in America. That was before petroleum displaced whale oil as the nation's fuel for illumination. Fisheries and manufacturing took the place vacated by whaling, but the decline of manufacturing during the last century led to a loss of prestige, and it now had a gritty reputation.

There are pockets of elegant homes in such communities, and New Bedford has a larger selection than most, possibly because it is the county seat of Bristol County, with associated courts and lawyers, and also because there is a large general hospital with a supporting medical community.

The house I had seen in the magazine was large, with enough space for Lorna's studio, a library, and a study for me, as well as guest rooms for our children when they came to visit. It had eight fireplaces. It was a very attractive house, and well maintained, in an area of similar homes.

I made an offer the same day. It was accepted, and eight days later I sold the house I had lived in for more than forty years. Lorna and I moved in together, and were married the following June. A hundred and ten relatives and friends gathered for the ceremony that we held in our new front hall.

THE END